T0146597

I am co-creator

Live.
Intensely.
Fully.
Eternally.

Mabelle Wilsi

BALBOA
PRESS

A DIVISION OF HAY HOUSE

Balboa Press books may be ordered through booksellers or by contacting:

Balboa Press
A Division of Hay House
1663 Liberty Drive
Bloomington, IN 47403
www.balboapress.com
1 (877) 407-4847

Print information available on the last page.

ISBN: 978-1-5043-6787-5 (sc)
ISBN: 978-1-5043-6788-2 (e)

Library of Congress Control Number: 2016917036

Balboa Press rev. date: 10/25/2016

Contents

Preface

- To all the amazing beings I meet on my path. To all the people who come and go in my LIFE

- To my father Assou Wilsi for being such an amazing teacher and an example throughout my LIFE and for becoming my guide and angel guardian in the afterlife. Love you forever Papa.

- To my mother Navi, through whom I came on this planet. Thank you mum for allowing me in your womb. Through your courage and strong will, you taught me that I can become who I want to be no mater the circumstances.

- To the beautiful angels in my LIFE:

   Faby Biquet, author of 'Mon evolution par l'Amour". Thank you for all the time you held the space for me so I could open up without feeling judged and for letting me figure out my OWN answer.

   Indra Perry for becoming my "sister". Thank you for the long walks and for always being there when I needed to share a part of my life, and for allowing me to be part of your family Life. It is amazing that we bonded so deeply and to, always being in connection. I love you forever beautiful Angel.

Thank you to my biggest teachers; every one of my eight siblings. I am grateful to have you as brothers and sisters: Grand-Frère, Samson, Nanan, Coko, Louez, Anyo, Majoie and Agbé. I love you as you are, magnificent beings of light.

Big thanks to my ancestors who have always assisted and continue to assist and guide me daily. I wouldn't be here without you. I acknowledge you in my LIFE.

Foreword

LIFE. What is life?

How can I impact my own life to make every day worth of being lived?

How do I get the answers to all the questions I ask myself?

How can I reel on my thoughts and bring forth the type of LIFE I want to live?

It is the story of who I was, who I am and who I aspire to become.

The words come on their own. One word at the time, eventually it becomes an amazing story, an amazing story of my personal growth, my realization and the love for the magnificent being I AM.

May part of this book or the entire book inspire you on your OWN very UNIQUE life path.

At the end of each chapter, you have the opportunity to write part of your own story.

With love
Mabelle Wilsi.

Introduction

I met Mabelle when she was studying. She came often to the old farm where I live and she helped with gardening and cooking.

She smiled and laughed all the time. She was a helper and a shoulder for everyone. Really! Her teachers, her friends, people around her always appreciated her presence, her way of being.

Mabelle seemed always happy and without worries… And she never really spoke about herself, about her life and about her past. I could feel a certain contrast between her outside world and her inner difficulties to meet herself. She needed time to learn about herself through Life experiences…

She jumped into the unknown, into Life… She – again – found courage and enough confidence to go where her soul pushed her. And she succeeded every time in exploring life and to observing her own way. I'm sure she will continue that way… Her way!

Both we go on through our own life's experiences and we share our spiritual growths by Skype and e-mails. Thank you to those technologies which didn't exist when I was Young… We meet from time to time but Love remains like we live under the same roof.

I hope you enjoy her story (I do!) and that it could inspire you on your own Life Journey!

I am grateful I know Mabelle, I am grateful to be able to share with her who we are, I am grateful to be her friend!

Faby Biquet
Author of
"Mon evolution par l'amour"

Chapter One

Present

*"Be present in my LIFE, allow it to
nourish that power within."*
"I co-create. IAM"
*"I learn from everyone I meet on my path
and from every situation I encounter in my life"*
"Live Intensely Fully Eternally"
"I am breathing; I am present; all falls in place"

Be present in my life; allow it to nourish that power within. Work with my feminine energy, accept it. I co-create, I am.

I ask myself how I can stay grounded in everyday life. The desire to stay grounded is constantly present, but then there are times where I'd rather be in my head, avoiding situation or not listening to the person in front of me "because s-he is annoying".

The truth is I learn from everyone I meet on my path. What in this person is annoying me so much?

I was going to a meditation class. I decided to park on the side of the road, there was a car behind me; I forgot to put the signal, but I drove my car to the right, to leave him enough room to pass it. He didn't see it that way. He drove up to the same level as my car and waited for me to turn toward him. I was busy unbuckling my seat belt and getting the manual I needed for the course. Maybe it took a minute. When I turn, ready to get out of the car, he was still there and had an angry face. I have no idea what he was saying, I couldn't hear it, and I didn't waste any energy trying to read his lips.

My 1st thought was "man, you really need to meditate, maybe you need to come to this class with me". He passed me, and I went to the course. During the course I was imagining myself having super power, like being able to run really fast. I was imagining myself running beside his car, stopping it, and making him come to the meditation class so he can understand that he doesn't need to be angry. Those thoughts left me smiling.

I learned not to take someone else's anger, misery or depression personally, as I used to do.

I learned how to breathe.

Yes I know, I breathe every day, big deal. We all do, but how conscious am I of my breath? It is natural, so I often forget that I am even breathing, until I stop and take a deep breath that fill up my lungs and exhale, emptying my lungs completely. I feel right away grounded when I do so, I am more present in what I am doing. And if I am still finding the person in front of me so annoying, then I observe that person more, and I see beyond the person. I no longer have in front of me a woman or a man, I have a perfect being, and that always makes me smile. I have a perfect being who is sharing some of their life experience, story with me, what an honour! Should I decide that I don't like the energy that surrounds that perfect being, I can, CONSCIOUSLY, choose to end the conversation without judgment, with love and compassion.

When stressful situation arises, what is a stressful situation? It is a "situation or factor causing a physical, mental or emotional tension".

What makes a situation stressful?

What I came to realize is that I feel stressed when I have expectation, when I have hope, when in my head it needs to be a certain way. So when it doesn't turn out the way I wanted it to turn out, I am stress. When I follow someone else's gut, and I am not aligning with the universe or don't follow my truth I am stressed. "Now Esther, what do we do?" I'll find myself asking myself.

Breathing. As simple as that. Being aware of my reality, to what is happening out there, if I want to call that reality.

Breathing brings me to the present moment. I found it impossible to be taking deep breaths and projecting myself in the future or living an event that happen in the past. I am fully in my body. Well I chose to do this journey in a physical body; I might as well enjoy it while it lasts. I am more aware of how I land my feet on the ground, how I hold that beautiful body of mine.

Breathing connects me to the core of the Universe, the Divine, and the Source and especially keeps me grounded on mother earth. I am grounded; I leave my head and stay connected.

The answers come easier, because all I am doing is breathing; I am no longer trying to figure out everything. I am breathing, I am present, and all falls in place exactly as it needs to.

I am co-creator

_____

_____

_____

_____

_____

_____

_____

_____

_____

_____

_____

_____

_____

_____

_____

_____

_____

_____

_____

_____

_____

I am co-creator

_____

_____

_____

_____

_____

_____

_____

_____

_____

_____

_____

_____

_____

_____

_____

_____

_____

_____

_____

_____

_____

_____

Chapter Two

Love

"I am here on earth to support and love myself deeply"
"I learn to express myself without expecting anything"
"I learn at my own pace"
"It is through the small habits that we build our love"
"My heart is big enough to love again"
"I am creating smaller habits with myself"

LOVE: *a profoundly tender, passionate affection for another person.*

2. a feeling of warm personal attachment or deep affection, as for a parent, child, or friend.

3. sexual passion or desire. (1–The random house dictionary)

Noun: An intense feeling of deep affection

Verb: Feel a deep romantic or sexual attachment to (someone)

Here was my definition of love:

He will love you when the sun goes down
And hate you when the sun comes up
Because he is a man, don't you know?

He will cheer with you when he succeeds
And blame you when he fails
Because he is a man don't you know?

He will avoid your comments during the day
And lay on you, in you when comes dusk
Because he is a man, don't you know?

You will pick up after him
You will do the laundry, fold
and put his cloths away
Because you are a woman, don't you know?

You will cook him delicious meals
You will provide for him when
he chooses not to work
Because you are a woman, don't you know?

Your mother took care of your dad
Your mother was a strong woman
Your mother never cried in front of anyone
Because she is a woman, don't you know?

You will only show your happiness
You will bury deep your sorrow
Because you are a woman, don't you know?

You will be strong and soft at the same time
You will be his wife, his friend
His lover and his mother at the same time
Because you are a woman, don't you know?

You will kneel when you are asked to
You will allow his semen in you
Because you are a woman, don't you know?

You will bury your emotions
You will be present and happy at all time
Because you are a woman, don't you know?

Your mother is a woman
Your grandma was a woman before your mother
And in their footprints you will step
Because you are a woman, don't you know?

I searched the Internet for: "How many times does a person fall in love in their life?" Of course, there were many answers. One answer that appeared many times made me jump, "Once" it said, "If it is the real one" it said.

What does "The Real One" mean?

I fell in love three times—True love, unconditional love.

A friend said that it was not possible nowadays to meet someone who will love us unconditionally. I said:

"I have loved unconditionally"

"And what happened?" he asked.

"It was painful. I was expecting the same from the other person."

He laughed. I then realized that I didn't love those men unconditionally, because I had expectations, and as long as there are expectations attached to the love I had for them, I could not call it unconditional. Expectations and unconditional love do not go hand in hand.

Expectations=Deceptions.

I am over thirty, and I fell in love only three times? Is it too much or not enough? What is too much or not enough?

I fell in love three times and they were each the real one for me.

My first love

My first love was the love I had for my dad, a true genuine love that was emanated from my heart, a love that will fill all my being anytime "papa" got home from work. What a pleasure to see him walk in the house. That love had some fear to it as well, especially those days where I disrespected him. I remember, at the beginning of his disease, I was 12; he was sitting in the TV room on the 1 seat couch, he needed an extra cushion, and requested mine; well as a teenager, I decided that it was in my right not to give it to him. Knowing that I wasn't going to win that battle, I threw it at his face. He grabbed it just before it hit his face and just stared at me. I didn't know where to put myself in order to escape that gaze.

I eventually left the room without looking back once, well, the movie no longer matter, my sanity did.

Even though I had that fear toward my dad that a simple look from him made me run out of a room, the love I had for him was much bigger, but then he "left". Eventually he passed away from the disease he had for 2 years. I was still a teenager at a time, an age I needed my papa more than anything. At that age where I had many questions.

My first unconditional love, my biggest lost, my first lost. The first time I was "dumped". How can I trust enough to fully let my heart be taken by another man? How can I fully trust enough to allow myself to just give that unconditional love to another man when the first man who I gave that love to, left me without saying goodbye when

I needed him the most? How do I get out of that spiral of wanting to love unconditionally and being scared of doing it? Maybe, I can only have one big love in my life, and that love is the one I have for my dad.

Then there was Sun.

I was on a trend of my life as a single woman. I was able to convince myself that I was happy that way and mostly that I didn't want to love a man anymore. "He will, too leave me when I will need him the most" I didn't want any man in my life.

We recognized each other the first time we saw each other—we just knew. We went to each other and spent the whole night talking like two old friends who missed each other. We spent hours talking; we had so much to share. It felt that we lived a past life together and were glad to be together again.

I felt comfortable around him; I felt like I no longer needed the walls I put up high after the loss of my first love. I brought those walls down. I allowed myself to be happy with a man, to trust him and to do the scariest thing: open up my heart and let him in. We quickly discovered that we had the same dream: to open an orphanage in a Country in West Africa, in Gambia, and to adopt a girl, our daughter.

At times a look at each other said what we were thinking. Words were no longer needed. We argued often. That was new to me. Being in love, loving someone meant that I needed to embrace the other point of view, meant that we should be on the same page at all time

Before that, I could never get upset. It didn't matter what was happening. I might get annoyed, which would last five minutes at the most. I had never been able to express my feelings, everything was hidden inside.

Mother used to say, "Mabelle never gets mad, you can do whatever you want to her, she will come back within minutes and talk to you and won't even mention the issue."

Does that mean that I was a great kid? No, it just meant that I pushed all my feelings and emotions down, and I believed that I wasn't worth being loved. I thought if I became upset, I might lose the only people who loved me. It was the truth for me. It was my truth.

This is the definition of my truth:

Whatever I believed in unequivocally is my truth.

Several lies were considered truth because several people believed in them. Ancient Greeks and Babylonians believed that the earth was a flat disc. Romans believed that the earth was at the center of the universe and that the sun revolves around it. In the later centuries, it was believed that babies didn't feel pain.

When I met Sun, a door, doors, of emotion opened up. Something happened within me that I was able to allow myself to cry in front of him, to feel sadness and to express it. I was able to express the beginning of anger quickly and then smile again. I was surprised; I didn't know what to do with all of those emotions that came up. I didn't know how to handle them. I had never received an instruction manual on "how to deal with your emotions in twelve steps". I didn't know what was happening.

I asked myself, "Where do all these tears come from? How come I cry when I am sad?" Then, I told myself, "This is insane. This is not me at all.

It has to be Sun. It is his fault I feel these emotions. I'll tell him how miserable he makes me."

I cried the day my dad passed because my mum was crying, and it made me sad to see my mother cry.

At his funeral I let out a loud, sad scream and that was it for the rest of the day. And for most of my life until I met Sun, there were no more tears.

"What to do with all those tears, why don't they stop when I ask them to?" I asked myself over and over again.

Not knowing what was happening, I convinced myself that Sun was doing something wrong to me. It had to be his fault. Instead of telling him, "Love, I've never felt that emotional before. I am confused and don't know how to deal with it. Support me in expressing my emotions in a healthier way." I said, "See, you make me sad again. I've never cried like this before. This is your fault."

Every single tear was his fault.

STOP! No one can ever make me do something or make me feel a certain way. I choose to do whatever I am doing and feel the way I am feeling.

Even if today I feel sad and unhappy the whole day, I am the one who chose those feelings.

It is not my mother, my ex-boyfriend or the waitress that made me angry, but instead it is an old feeling or emotion that hasn't been resolved. The anger is resurfacing in order for me to deal with it, so I can move on and not be trapped in the same spot forever; a kind of awareness.

I also realized that I am not alone in a relationship, I have the other, my partner, who is a reflection of where I was in my life at the moment. I met him and we chose to be together.

Choosing to give all my attention to my partner and forgetting about myself is not healthy. We are two, YOU and ME forming US. YOU alone do not form US, and I alone do not form US. I need to exist in the relationship, express myself, my desires, my truth. This doesn't mean he will agree with me. If I feel like cuddling and just BEING, he might think about going for a movie instead.

I often forgot to express myself, to get my voice out of my throat, say my truth. If I felt like going to the sea to spend a weekend together, I would barely say it. I would wait, expecting him to read my mind. And instead of the sea, I would find myself drinking in a bar with him and his friends. It was quite the opposite of my desire, but I figured that it was alright.

What happens when I suppress my feelings too much? Eventually, I burst. That is normal. I cannot keep filling a balloon with air and expect it to grow larger with no consequences. It will certainly burst. As a child, I did this several times. I blew into a balloon until it burst; it was a game I played quite often.

But not knowing how to express anger healthily, I didn't burst. I kept taking in more and more. I didn't know what else to do, but even the time I felt the anger, I didn't have the words to express it; the feeling of not being understood stayed in me.

But with Sun, I discovered that we could disagree and still love each other. Arguments didn't seem to dull the love I had for him. It made me grow closer to him. I started feeling comfortable with my emotions and slowly, I learned to express my anger, first by writing. It was easier for me as I didn't have to see him when he read the note. I will leave him a note, most of the time it was a letter. After he read it, we will sit and discuss it.

The words come clearly when I write to express my feelings and mention the subject of disagreement. The most amazing part of writing is that I keep learning more and more about myself as well. I learn how to handle different situations that arise in my life.

Learning to express my anger truly opened doors. Opening those doors helped me cleanse some old anger and allowed me to learn to express my emotions in a healthier way. Realizing the problem, identifying it, helped me let go without blame.

French is my first language, it was his third language. We were up in his apartment; after we had supper, I congratulated him at the fact that his French was improving so well. "Thank you, at least I make some effort in French, you don't even speak my language and don't even show any interest in learning it". It became a fight. He was mad and I couldn't see why. I started watching subtitled Dutch movie. It made him happy even if I couldn't understand a single word; it was a step forward to understanding and speaking Dutch one day.

Then in the breaking up, there was no fight. We both knew it was no longer working and we both needed to move on. Despite that knowing, I was devastated. A part of me felt betrayed, if he was the real one, he had to work out. After that morning conversation that sealed the end of the relationship, I lay on the couch with the television on; I was staring at the ceiling. I lay on that couch for the entire day. At night I went to bed. And that was my life for the next four days. On the living room table, I had a bottle of apple juice, the only "food" I was able to stand. The television was on, my gaze on the ceiling. I had no idea how I was going to pick up the pieces, my pieces. I felt apart. I kept all within close to my heart; it was like a sharp precious stone that was tearing my heart apart, that was tearing my whole being apart.

But I refused to share the story with anyone. I refused to share my hurt with anyone, because I was scared that by doing so I would have completely lost him. I was scared that letting go, even a tiny bit of this story would have been letting go a part of him. It was my hurt, my own very hurt. I deserved it; I kept it within me with pride, a wound I was the only one to see, a deep wound that wasn't sewn and left an ugly scare, but a scare I was wearing with pride.

My body reacted in a very strange manner. The reaction made me begin listening more to my body, making the connection between my feelings and my physical, external reactions.

Every evening my body will become covered with rashes, I scratched myself like a mad woman, again and again, until sleep became my saviour. The first time it happened, I planned to see a doctor in the morning, thinking it was an allergic reaction. But in the morning, my skin was clean. There was nothing that could remind me of the previous night's scratching. It was as if nothing happened the night before, and I thought maybe it was just a bad dream.

It was not a dream, and the rash continued every night for two months until eventually I had to focus on the cause of the rash beyond the physical level. I mean, I couldn't go and see a doctor in the morning and tell him yesterday evening I was covered with rashes, but they're all gone this morning. Only two things could have happened, either he would prescribe me any kind of cream or find me a psychological disease. So I decided to pay attention to when the rashes appeared.

Whenever I felt unworthy, when I felt the relationship ended because of me, that he was too good for me, that I was useless, the rash appeared. Whenever I felt taken advantage, when I thought of him sleeping with my friend, the rashes appeared; and I would scratch myself. So whenever those thoughts popped into my head, I stopped them right there, at the beginning. Soon, I started having rashes only on certain parts of my body, my legs, and my back. The rash no longer spread to my entire body anymore. I paid attention to my feelings until there were no more rashes at night.

I forgot too often about my dear, sweet self in the relationship.

I was raised to put other's needs before my own. My needs were always fulfilled second. And I brought that belief into that loving and passionate relationship. That relationship taught me that my desires are as important as my partner's. I learned that I can listen to my partner's desires and accept that it is not my responsibility to fulfill them. I learned to express myself without expecting anything from my partner. I learned that expressing feelings of anger and desire allow me to easily let go of those feelings instead of spending days daydreaming about what could have been.

Unconditional love is affection without any expectation. It is the type of love that is unchanging regardless of the situation or the conditions.

Unconditional love=No attachment. No expectation. No hope. No wishes. It's a LOVE that just IS.

After many years of avoiding the masculine gender; after many years of avoiding being touched by a man, I decided that "Esther it is may be time for you to meet someone?" It still took me time to fall out of love. I had to reopen the scar, so the wound underneath it could heal properly, in order for it to be properly sewn. The scar was, is still there, but it is smooth, the wound underneath it is completely healed.

When I look at that scar, when I caressed it, it reminded me that I know how to love and that I can be loved. It reminded me that I lived that story, and that there are never 2 stories that unfold the same way.

So, I kiss that scar, I thank it; it is the result of something strong that I lived, it is the result of the fusion between two beings, me and my soul mate.

If I go by the principle that I am the creator of my reality, that means that I welcomed that man in my life and chose to love him deeply. I learned from that relationship by taking steps that eventually brought the relationship to an end. I blamed him, yes, I did, but not for a long period of time. Then, being my worst enemy I blamed myself. I blamed my lack of trust in myself. I blamed the fact that I couldn't get mad at him.

There were days I sat, envisioned him, and said I love you, I love you, I love you, without any other thoughts, and certainly without expectations. Saying those words made me feel better; made me release a bit of him every day, allowed me to slowly feel no more anger toward him. I learned about who I was. More importantly, I learned it is ok to be upset and to say it.

When I realized all that I learned for being in the relationship with him, I sent him a message to thank him. I thanked him for being on my path, for being my teacher, for being my lover, mainly my teacher.

I am grateful for him.

My Third Love.

Oh well, again a learning process.

I needed to, still need to, learn to be patient. I had learned to be patient with myself, but I needed to learn to be patient with others. I had to keep in mind that we all have our own path, that we step into our power when it is our time—not when Esther says it is time.

I honestly thought that speaking my truth, which I thought must be his truth as well, right in front of his face, would change his way of seeing life. But no. My third love taught me that. He taught me what unconditional love is all about.

I am me with all my blockages, my past experiences, my beliefs, my fears, and my difficulties.

You are you with all your blockages, your present experiences, your difficulties, your past experiences, your fear and worries.

We met, we recognized something in each other and we decided to be together for as long as it lasted. By getting together, we brought our past relationships, our beliefs, fears, and blockages. It was not only HIM and I, it was HIM and I, our past relationships and our beliefs about life and love.

There can be many past people and experiences in one relationship. We bring all of those people with us when we build a new relationship. Hopefully we learn from each other and grow together. But what happens if we are not ready to let go of our past experiences? What happens if I cannot remove my winter jacket in full summer? You can tell me that it is sunny and warm, but it is up to me to remove the coat or to ask for your help if I cannot do it alone. But you cannot make me remove it. If I remove my coat just to make you happy, I guaranty you that as soon as we have a disagreement, I will put it back on for a longer period of time.

I learn at my own pace, and loving you means accepting that you learn at your own pace as well. If I find myself learning a bit faster than you and find myself in LIFE grade 5 while you are still in LIFE grade 2, with LOVE and through LOVE I will support you get to grade 5. However, if I see that you feel comfortable where you are at, from LOVE and through LOVE as well, I will set you free. I will let you continue learning at your own pace. I will put my personal growth and happiness before OUR growth and happiness. I will choose not to return to grade 2 with you, but instead learn the lesson I need to learn in grade 5 and continue on my journey. Who knows? Maybe in few years you will catch up and WE can be together again.

I realized that what was hard about moving on was not the knowledge of our unfulfilled dreams. It was not the broken hopes, the impossible future together. What was hard was breaking the small simple habits: seeing his car in the driveway; seeing his shoes thrown messily by the entrance and putting them away neatly for two years; being in the kitchen or doing some craftwork and seeing him walk by without a word; just being in his presence. Those small things became so significant. I understand now that those small habits make a relationship. It is through the small habits that we built our relationship: kissing good night, being the last to talk to at night, going to bed together (which

I lacked); holding hands. Yes, small habits created our relationship.

Small habits are making me miss a man that I know I can no longer share my life with. I am craving those small habits, and it hurts.

Christmas time has never meant much to me, being brought up Jehovah's Witness, it was another day, season in the year. But to have been part of his family, a family that values Christmas, I felt empty at that moment. I missed some family warmth, the sharing, the laughter, the games, the hugs. I missed those small habits.

All those small habits create LIFE, create LOVE, created a bond between him and I.

Those small habits became rarer and rarer, that bond became thinner and thinner to the point where it could no longer hold us together.

We grew apart.

Now I see the value of having those small habits in the relationship: morning walks, evening talks, morning hugs, evening cuddles, morning kiss good morning and good day, evening kiss welcome and good night, holding hands when walking or when sitting beside each other, pausing to look into each other's eyes when talking, by breathing when talking to each other we communicate instead of reacting with each other, talking to each other, unexpected gifts, weekend trips together, snuggles on the couch.

All of those small habits build a strong, a stronger love relationship.

I am grateful for the relationship. I am grateful I am able to understand it. I am grateful I can see the worth of small habits. I can take that knowledge to my next relationship.

Now, I choose to create small habits with myself, in order to have a healthier, stronger relationship with myself.

I create these small habits to care of myself emotionally, spiritually, physically, mentally and financially.

What I have learnt from the men I allowed to enter my heart, to fall in love with, is that love has multiple aspects. Loving another man doesn't take away any fragment of the love I have for my dad, it actually makes that love grow. How so? By feeling all the gratitude toward a man who taught me how to love by allowing me to love him and by showing me his love by spending time with me. I learnt from him that love never dies, it just changes form. I guess love is like energy, it can never be destroyed, but can only change form. So, I can never hate the men I loved, allowed in my life, that love actually transcended and I learnt more about myself, I learnt that my heart is big enough to accommodate loving a partner, and when the relationship doesn't go the way intended, and the relationship is completed, I still have lot of room left in my heart to allow another partner in my life, and that love needs not to step on the other one, but complete it and make my heart grow bigger and bigger.

Inside my heart I feel a big space that I fill every day with Joy, openness and light. From there I go to the other to "meet" him and to share our respective paths through Life.

When I choose to do something for my partner, it's to support him in his direction. It's more "a gift of love" to him. And a gift is not meant to be taken back... I have learned to say a real "no" and a real "yes" because I trust him to take care of himself.

I never know how long a relationship will last. And if I need or choose to end the relationship, it's never "against" my partner, it is "for us, our life path", and the energy of love survives and remains. And I leave the other with love!

And each relationship I live can be lived as "different and true experiences for both"

Each day is a brand new day and I may discover many things...or nothing, it might seem at time, but it is always my choice. I may choose to see Life through the eyes of the Heart or through my fears and desires only... It's just a BIG difference in experiencing Love...

I am co-creator

_____

_____

_____

_____

_____

_____

_____

_____

_____

_____

_____

_____

_____

_____

_____

_____

_____

_____

_____

_____

_____

_____

_____

_____

_____

_____

_____

_____

_____

_____

_____

_____

_____

_____

_____

_____

_____

_____

_____

_____

I am co-creator

_____

_____

_____

_____

_____

_____

_____

_____

_____

_____

_____

_____

_____

_____

_____

_____

_____

_____

_____

_____

_____

_____

Chapter Three

My Truth

*"I just live LIFE and take a full
bite of every moment"*
"My power ends at me expressing my truth"
*"By loving someone, I learn about
accepting that person"*
"My journey now is to communicate"
*"The truth is LIFE is here. It is like
the air I choose to breath"*

"Love doesn't need to be overwhelming" he says

I smile.

"I know, but I don't know how to feel love a different way"

When I feel love, it's always intense. I asked myself this question:

"Do I feel love so intensely because I think I am not worth being loved or because I think I need to give all of my soul to love?"

I'll take the second one, that's what reflects me, the most.

Maybe my backgrounds, maybe the way I have been raised; "have only one lover and give all your love to that one and only one man, your spouse".

I am not married; I had few lovers, and I gave all my love to couple of them, all the love I was able to feel within me.

"Why did you say yes? You should have told him that you are busy and that you can't see him on the week end" My sister said.

"And why will I do that, when actually I want to see him on the week end, why pretend and say something that's not true?" I asked

"You're way too easy" she replied.

I am confused; so in order for me to be loved or respected in a relationship, I need to pretend? I am not sure if that's how it works.

I often follow my intuition, I don't go around it or pretend that it is not right in front of my face, or ignore the feeling of a situation not being right for me or that it's not the right time to do something. I go ahead and don't question it, but according to my sister and some friends, I need to pretend in order to be loved by someone, I need to make myself "inaccessible", so "he can run" after me.

Hard to do for me. If I feel like seeing you, I will say yes; if I don't feel like seeing you for whatever reason, I will say no, and not feeling obligated to explain myself other than "I just don't feel like".

But love's "instruction manual" is different than how I live my life. So I said "screw it, if I have to pretend in order to be loved and accepted as I am in a relationship, oh well I guess I won't be with anyone then".

I love you, you love me, or at least we like each other, let sit and take time to know each other, period. We both want to be together, let make the time and know each other, period. What is so scaring about? What? I seem not to see it.

I am here, right now; let say I pretend, I want to see you, but then I say no, find whatever excuses possible, my dog giving birth today or I will be busy the whole day working in the garden or so one. So today, I have the opportunity to see you; today I have the time to see you, but I choose not to, not because I am busy, but just because I want you to believe that I am not "easy". There is this say "tomorrow might never come". It is not being fatalist, or seeing life all in dark, but that's reality. All I know, is that now I am breathing and I am healthy and still in my physical form, tomorrow I don't know where I might, will be. I plan, yes I plan, but whatever happen will happen. There are other forces outside of me, outside of "my little world" that operate, and that's what it is.

So let me tell you that I am busy today, just so you can think that I am inaccessible, but eventually I will be accessible. So I will spend time, time that we can spend together, to "resist" you. And at the end, we might be together and I will regret not spending the time I could have spent with you, and if we are not, I will say "Lucky enough that I "resisted" him otherwise we would have broken up and would have been sad". But there is another version of that. I don't "resist" you, I do not pretend that I am busy exactly the day and time you ask me to go out for a drink, and eventually at the end we might still be together, and then I'll tell myself "Great I didn't waste time, but took advantage of the time I had and spent it with you" and if it happens that we don't end up being together, I will say to myself "I lived, 2,3 days of intense love, felt loved and share something with someone, I received and learnt exactly what I needed to" and LIFE goes on. No regrets. Do not want to live my life with lot of "I could have or should have done this or that".

So I just live LIFE and take a full bite of every moment. There are times where it is not easy at all, times where I get, let myself get caught in a drama, most of the time going on in my head, in a "trying to guess what the other is thinking".

I need to constantly remind myself that I bring forth the experiences that arise in my life, that people I bring into my life are a reflection of what is within me. It is me in them, them in me, we are all one.

I stood in front of the bathroom mirror, after an appointment with a friend has been cancelled without any word being said, he just didn't show up, being more and more annoyed and mad and crying on my little self, "my poor me". Eventually my voice broke through all those emotions and asked "why do you keep bringing those experiences, those relationships in your life? If you don't want to experience this type of relationship, oh well let go of it" LET GO OF IT, BE WILLING to let go of it.

Of course I want to let go of it, of course I want to create relationship where I am fully respected as an individual and where we can communicate effectively, but how come this is not happening? "Fully respected" "Communicate effectively", 2 big words that I never applied in most of my life. I couldn't even be able to define those words, but that what I want to bring forth in my life. Well, now that I am aware of it, it means it is at the conscious level, so let go and find that relationship. But then I slip back and I bring in my life relationship where there is no communication, so I go through that stage of "no one understand me or loves me, what's wrong with me?"

Old patterns. I find situation that will trigger my old way of thinking, to go back to this that I am used to, to that old "comfortable" way of living, my sweet comfort zone, regardless if it is healthy, still serve the life I want to live or not. It is comfortable because I am used to it.

And I am annoyed,

"Why do I keep bringing the same type of experience in my life, why? I got it, ok LIFE, I got it, I got the lesson, but then why you keep throwing the same stuff at me?" Life might mistake me for someone else.

And it hits me, it hits me. I am learning how to communicate, and every day I am communicating more and more effectively, where I know that I am the subject, there is no more "you make me feel this way or do this…", there are more of "I feel, I felt". But then I can express myself, my emotions, only that anytime I think that I am not heard, I am annoyed. "Why do you ask me my point of view, why did you ask me how I feel if you are not hearing me?"

Now the true question is

"How important for me is it to be heard?"

I want to communicate effectively, I am doing it for me, for my own personal growth, can I make the other listen, hear me?

My power ends at **me expressing my truth.** I said it! The other decides what he wants to do with it. Expressing myself, is expressing my truth it is not waiting for an approval from the other; so I communicate more freely. I communicate, I say how I felt, I feel, get it out of my chest, put it out there. It is my path for me to learn, to learn not to take it personally when I feel misunderstood. To learn to be open and not to wait for the other to reply the way I wanted him to do so, to suit the movie in my head and make me right.

My journey now is to communicate and I did it. That's it.

The way the other respond is her journey, is her path, it has nothing to do with me.

I am here on earth to support and love myself so deeply that all the thoughts I have about myself are filled with love, joy and truth and accept myself fully as I am. And that's what I am doing by saying my truth. And it should not take an ounce of the love I feel toward myself if it falls in depth ear.

I am here to learn from my experience and from others.

My mum told me quite often that life is too short to be able to experience everything and make all mistakes that there are to make and that is why I have this person in front of me, who has more experiences or made mistakes I can learn from without having to ever experience them.

I am telling the stories I want to tell, I am telling the stories I want them to believe, that I want them to think it is true.

I asked my guide:

"Why, why do I keep attracting the same kind of people in my life"

The answer was quick, as a human being I was impressed by the speed at which the answer came, as they were just waiting for me to ask it.

"You need to learn, 1ˢᵗ of all you need to remember that whatever that's happening out there happens, the way you react to it make those people you meet on your path who you believe they are. A situation happen, let say someone just said that you are overweight, the way you react to it will make you stick to the statement: I always attract the same kind of person in my life. So if

anytime you hear that statement you get mad, or sad, that means there is more work, from your part to be done on that level, so that situation will keep happening over and over and over again in your life until you get it, until the time when that statement will mean nothing for you, and that you might even be able to smile at that kind of statement, forget about it and go on your daily activities, so the question is not why you keep attracting the same kind of people in your life, but instead 'what can I do, how can I reel on my thoughts in order to attract the type on people I would like in my life?', and 'how can I let go when a situation or relationship no longer serves any purpose in my life?', those are the real questions".

What can I say to that? So I asked myself the "real question" and the answers were just so simple; I went back as far as I could to when I started attracting the type of people I would like not to have in my life, what are the feelings behind. All kind of emotions came up, especially the emotion of "I am so not worthy, I can't do anything positive in my life, I just can't do anything that will turn out right in my LIFE", and of course my 1st reaction was to blame my parents, oh daddy if you were this and you mummy if you were that, and started making a scenario in my head. Hold on, stop right now missy, as I said before, my parents did what they knew at the time, they did what they knew, period, I cannot change anything, they are who they are and I am who I am, if they projected their fears on me, if they wanted me to live the life they wanted for themselves, if they "knew everything" and I had to be quiet and listen when I was kid, it was all they knew, it was the way they knew to raise me. All they did was from a place of love, it might not be the place of love I wanted them to come from, but they did, and nothing I could do about it, yes one thing, thank them and now live the life I want for myself. Yes I have all those beliefs I learnt from them, or that I learnt at certain moment of my life, and those beliefs helped me at those moments of my life.

I had the belief that I cannot trust anybody. That belief came from the fact that I got laugh at few times when I open up to my parents or sometimes siblings, so slowly I started closing up. That statement help me at time when I was confused and I didn't know what the next step was;

"should I stay in Montreal, a city where I don't feel I can live up to my gifts or move to another city where all I know is where it is on a map?". Because of the past belief of "I cannot trust anybody", I started learning to ask my question to the universe, the Divine; even if at that moment I wasn't aware of it. I will ask, "show me a sign as where to go", and the sign will come. I talk to people about my desire to move out of Montreal, they gave me their point of view, and the same city came over and over. The fact the people I talk to were just clients of where I was working, it was easier for me to hear the message, because I had no attachment to them and they didn't try to force their point of view on me; they will tell me what they think about different cities in Canada and it was left to me to decide where to go.

My trust in the universe grew, as I knew that if I ask a clear question, the answer will be come, I just need to be open to the way it will come to me, and listen.

I often found myself imagining the way the answer will come to me and what the answer will be, so when the answer actually does come, I do not recognize it as the answer to my question, so I keep waiting and getting frustrated at the universe. Later one, I realize that I received the answer some time ago.

I have decided to take a course in the renewable energy. So I asked "is it my path to work in the renewable energy?" I have a close friend who gave me her opinion as she did not believe that I would be happy in that field, so to take the time and think about it. Being a close friend I didn't pay attention to it. So I asked for more sign. And here is the answer I got "if you are not enrolled in the course for the spring intake it is not for you", thank you.

The spring intake was full, I got enrolled in the fall intake, and I took the course. I remember how everything got difficult, from having the financial help to the place to live. Every single step was taking energy out of me, I was drained, sad most of the time, I was living in a dirty place, where I had to bleach out the bathroom anytime I needed to use it. I understood the answer to late, I finished the program, took the time to meet new people, took some activities I wanted to take. I will not say I wasted my time, as I learnt, I learnt to pay more attention to the answers to my questions, and accept them no matter the way they come through. I had to learn the most difficult part, to not think the answer will be what I want it to be, because honestly, as a human, how far can I see?

I remember my first premonitory dream.

My dad has been sick for over two years now, he finally undergone a surgery that made it better for some times, but then he needed to be admitted to the hospital again, just something minor, his surgeon said.

One Monday, we schedule to all go visit him; the hospital wasn't that close to home. That Monday early in the morning I woke up and stay in bed, it was too early. I woke up with a feeling of quietness knowing that it was all over. All I knew is that I was with my dad spirit, he was peaceful. I couldn't be sad, he was in peace, I couldn't be happy, it was a sad moment; I was confused, no one to talk to about. We went to the hospital, visited him, I left early, while everyone was still there, I couldn't look at him in the eyes, those eyes that were following me when I was going back and forth in the room, those eyes staring at me. Let me tell you a bit about my dad's eyes. He had a really expressive looks, and when he looked at me, I sometimes believed that he could see through me, it was impossible to lie to my dad, he will just lock his eyes on me and just that look will make me feel uncomfortable. And that was the look he had that day. I didn't know better at that time, I didn't know what to do, so I left, I left because I didn't want to see those eyes locked on me, I left without saying good bye, I just told my mother that I wasn't feeling well, that I needed to go home and rest, what I did; I went home and slept the whole day, I cried, I slept. I stayed in bed the whole day. 3 days later, he left his body, came and paid me a last visit when he visited me in the room he used to stay in when he was sick, my sister and I were staying in that room. He came, stood in the middle of the room, he was so peaceful, there was no more pain, him in a sublime light, just being, he stood there, I looked at him frightened and eventually fell back asleep. And that was it.

I didn't know what it was, especially that I have been brought up not to believe in spirit, "spirits are the work of the devil", I was more and more confused and learnt to be quiet about it after sharing it and being laughed at.

I kept experiencing dreams that turn out to happen in reality.

The last time I did experience dream about death, it was in one of my sibling family, around them; she just had her 1st child, not being able to interpret the dream as it came, I told her that I see death in her family. What a silly thing to say to a woman who just gave birth. Her sister in law passed away in the following week.

Knowing my gift, she, later told me that she couldn't leave her baby alone, she was constantly afraid that death will take him from her.

I decided to shut myself, what a curse, what a gift at the same time. Knowing that I caused that much worries, made me feel sad.

Those dreams come as feelings. I interpret the feelings, there are no words. Spirits don't use words, they use images, feelings. In my case it was feelings and a deep sense of knowing.

So maybe I could see far, but then nothing I could do to change the situation. It was like receiving a letter that tells you "you will be fired in 2 days, the decision has been taken, you have 2 days to get your stuffs together and say bye to your co-workers". That basically what it was. I had 3 days to say bye to my dad, or just be with my dad and enjoy those last moments with him.

I did exactly what I knew at that time, I was frightened, I went and "locked" myself in my bedroom and slept, maybe I slept hoping that it won't happen, maybe I slept hoping that I can go back to that dream and undo what was happening, or maybe that help me to cop out with his death before it happened; in any case I run away from reality and seek refuge in my sleep. And that was all I knew. So I am in the wrong position to point finger at my mother for not doing this or that this way or that way. I am in the wrong position. And if the way she lives her life doesn't suit me, oh well guess what, it is her life; now if I let the way she lives her life step in the way I live my life, then it is my responsibilities to do something about it or not, but again in the respect of the way she lives her life. I can simply tell her: "mum I love you and I know you are trying to help me by telling me how I should live my life, but it is my life and I would like to live it as I please, I will surely come and ask you for advices when I need to, but for now, I don't need any advice, but thank you". And that is. If she keeps trying I will keep repeating myself. "I don't tell you how to live your life and do not criticize how you live your life, so I am asking you to respect the way I live my life, not to agree with, but to respect it, and leave me alone making my own decision".

It takes time and patience. It can eventually become "all my other kids love me, you are the only kid who doesn't" and that's alright, we don't all have to have the same definition of love.

Wait a minute, what is love?

I turn to the bible to seek a definition. I have been brought up Christian and the bible was part of my daily life growing up. In Corinthians 13:4-7, it is defined as being kind; love bearing all things, hoping all things, enduring all things.

Nowhere do they define love as doing what you tell me to do or living my life according to your understanding of life. If loving you means letting go of all my beliefs about life, stop learning on my own and following exactly your path, then I am alright you telling me that I don't love you if I don't do all these, because I know that loving someone goes beyond that. And I still love you.

Isn't by loving someone the best gift I can give myself? Isn't by loving someone that I learn about accepting others as they are without judgment or criticism? What do I know, really about that person? Even about my mother, what do I know about her? Not much really. She can tell me how she suffered when her own dad passed away, she can tell me how she suffered when she lost her 2nd child at a young age, she can tell me how much she suffered caring for my dad until he passed; all I can do is nod; I can say "I am sorry to hear that, that sucks", I cannot live the hurt she lived, I cannot feel how she felt it.

It is her experience, her life experience and I know that it doesn't have to be mine. I am living my life experience now. If she is depressed because of those experiences, I don't have to take her depression on me and feel depressed for her, I don't even need to feel bad for her, I can, as healthy as it is for me to listen to her, to give her my opinion if she asks for, knowing that giving my opinion doesn't mean that she will do it as I said, even if it seems like a great idea for me, it might not be a great idea for her at that moment; or I can choose neither, and ask her to talk about something more constructive, she can refuse to do so, then we can just share a quiet moment together.

Like I said, I tell the stories I want to tell and the way I want to tell them, embodied in those stories are my life experiences. If I think that all in life suck, so those stories will reflect the bitterness I have toward life.

The truth is life is there. It is like the air. I have air around me, I choose to breathe, no one is making me. Air is not to blame if I stop breathing.

The same with life, I choose to live, and life did nothing wrong to me. I hear people say, "life's throwing challenges to me, but it hadn't beaten me down yet". Why will life be throwing challenges at me? Do I create those challenges myself or is life having fun and picking on me?

My thoughts, the decisions I make can turn out as challenges in my life or can turn out as blessings in my life or those challenges can become blessings in my life.

As soon as I realize that a situation no longer work for my well-being, I observe my thoughts, observe the type of decisions I have been making in my life and where those decisions brought me, then I can change what I no longer want in my life. I can choose to let go of relationship that no longer brighten my life or lift me up.

Oh yes, I can listen to you repeat the same stories over and over again, but I choose not to, I choose instead, as soon as you start telling the story to ask you "so what are you doing to make it better? What are you doing so your partner values you more?" Are you coming for a shoulder to cry on, every time you come and see me or are you coming to take charge of your life, vent it out, and tell the old stories so you can replace them with new, healthier stories? Why are you coming to me today for?

Not everyone should agree with me.

I joke often saying that I was a great kid, but don't ask my mum. Our points of views are slightly different. But that my point of views, and I don't want to agree to the one of my mother.

I support myself, and LIFE constantly supports me.

I am co-creator

_____

_____

_____

_____

_____

_____

_____

_____

_____

_____

_____

_____

_____

_____

_____

_____

_____

_____

_____

_____

_____

_____

_____

_____

_____

_____

_____

_____

_____

_____

_____

_____

_____

_____

_____

_____

_____

_____

_____

_____

_____

_____

I am co-creator

_____

_____

_____

_____

_____

_____

_____

_____

_____

_____

_____

_____

_____

_____

_____

_____

_____

_____

_____

_____

Chapter Four

Birth

"I am an amazing being. I am
complex, but yet simple"
"I am paying attention to that voice in my head"
"What I think or say I become"
"The fusion between two beings"
"I can choose to go or not"

Here is the story I told myself about my pre-life before earth.

I was sent to be born in a small town on a beach; it was a hot summer day.

I remember exactly how it happened.

It was a nice quiet afternoon, maybe too quiet! We were playing ball, teasing each other, laughing. It was my turn to throw the ball, and that is when SHE came.

"May I talk to you?"

"Of course you may. Hey guys remember, it is my turn to throw the ball, I will be back in a bit," I yelled to my pal

SHE walked ahead of me, faster than usual. I told myself that it must be a serious matter. I decided to follow HER without asking any question and let HER talk when SHE was ready.

I didn't know what to call HER, because mainly I don't remember. And that is what SHE told me first:

"You will not remember clearly, but I and all of this will be somewhere in the back of your head."

I still often search the back of my head, but absolutely nothing comes up.

She spoke, and I listened.

"What? Be sent into a crazy family of seven, no way, I am not ready for that."

"You know it would have happened."

"I know, but I thought I could choose."

"You always have the choice. You can choose to go or not."

"And what will happen if I choose not to go?"

"Nothing, you will go back to playing ball, and one day we will have the same conversation again."

I sat there, gazing at the vast space, all the beauty and joy around me. I was being asked to be sent to Earth, to be born into a crazy family of seven? I had been there before, I knew what it was.

Was I ready to do it all over again? I thought I could refuse this time, and maybe next time would never come. But I felt compassion at the same time, compassion for the parents of seven kids.

"Why do they need me?" I asked.

"The father is a great man with a great gift. He needs to pass that gift on to someone else before he leaves the planet."

"Perfect, I guess he already has lots of choices. There is no point in me going down there and making his choice more difficult. Problem solved, I am going back to the game. Can't he pass his gifts to any of his seven kids?"

"None of them will know how to use it. The gift will be spoiled, wasted. We don't like having a gift liked that floating in the universe, unused. You will hold that family together, you will provide support to that family, and you will be the one they can all rely on. You will be their eyes to Know, their mouth to speak the Truth, their heart to Love unconditionally."

"So, I will be a boy whose dad will love so much that he will be ready to share his gift with his son? That sounds like a great adventure."

"Yes, it can be a great adventure, only you will be a girl, and the dad will never show you his love and never tell you what he sees in you."

I sat for a moment, not sure what to do. But I quickly devised a test.

"I will stay only after they pass a test. Then, I will know that the dad really needs someone."

"What will the test be?"

"I will go and come back, only their love and their desire to have me will make me stay."

"Then go and have a safe journey filled with Love, Joy, Happiness and Abundance."

As I prepared for the transformation, I feared that I was leaving a wonderful space to go to revisit a place less wonderful that I had already visited many times.

SHE shouted at me:

"REMEMBER YOU CAN ALWAYS SUMMON ME WHEN YOU NEED ANY GUIDANCE"

That truth has floated in the back of my head as well.

I stepped into the vortex of the infinite, going down, changing form, and found myself in a small, constrained space. I just wanted to get out and scream.

"But you have to follow the process, you have to live every single transformation that will take place during the 280 days." I was told before leaving.

It was nine months of cramps and turning on myself.

After five months, I activated the test. The test was to go and come back. The doctors told the mother that the foetus wasn't developing properly, that she was going to have a severely mentally handicapped kid. The doctors advised her to terminate the pregnancy.

Her friends advised her the same; but she wasn't sure; having other children, and one being just over 2 at the time, she needed to decide, if for the sake of the other kids she was to have an abortion or let that "defective" foetus live and have a child that will require her attention all of her life.

The father decided that the process should continue, and the mother agreed.

And here I am 32 years later, trying to remember what was in the back of my head that I needed to remember. I am searching for the gift my dad passed to me; wanting desperately to reel it in from the universe and avoid wasting his gift.

I am co-creator

_____

_____

_____

_____

_____

_____

_____

_____

_____

_____

_____

_____

_____

_____

_____

_____

_____

_____

_____

_____

_____

_____

_____

_____

_____

_____

_____

_____

_____

_____

_____

_____

_____

_____

_____

_____

_____

_____

_____

_____

_____

I am co-creator

_____

_____

_____

_____

_____

_____

_____

_____

_____

_____

_____

_____

_____

_____

_____

_____

_____

_____

_____

_____

_____

_____

Chapter Five

I am the Director

"Living is all about intentions, daily intentions"
"The word obligation is fading
away from my vocabulary"
"I am accepting myself and enjoying
every minute I spend with myself"
"I am aware of my feelings and I am detached"

I just came from the theatre. It was a violent movie, classified *category, violent.* I wanted to watch a violent movie, and I was well served.

A violent movie? What is happening?

I usually watch movies based on true stories or cartoons and comics. But I wanted to watch a violent movie, and violent that movie was. I thought about leaving the theatre at one point, thinking to myself,

"That can't be, there is way too much violence in the movie. That's just getting ridiculous."

I stayed until the end mainly because I was with a friend, and also I wanted to know the end of the story. I wanted to know what was the whole purpose of that much violence and if the situation was going to change to a more peaceful one.

After the movie, I kept thinking about the ridiculousness of the violence. And from that statement, I continued on to, "Life is just ridiculous. What a ridiculous game." However, I caught my thoughts and asked myself, "What makes life a ridiculous game?"

First, I am holding the camera, so I possess the eyes that see through the lens. If I no longer like what see, I can shift the lens to a better image, a better scenario.

Second, what is happening out there is filtered through my perception, and I provide the explanation I want.

Third, I wrote, write, and will write the script. I can change the script at any time to have a more fulfilling, pleasing scenario.

If I find the movie, the game—life ridiculous, perhaps I need to make changes to my script. I can change the plot, the scene, even the stars of the movie in order to make the film I want to.

What does that involve?

At the beginning of this new journey, when I became aware of holding the camera and writing the script and, most importantly, giving myself permission to change the script, I broke ties from family members and friends that had become part of my extended family. I never thought I would have been able to function without them in my life, never thought that I would recover from not talking to them as often as I used to, not sharing the joy, sorrow and accomplishment in my life with them.

How could I go from calling my family and friends once a week to calling them only when I felt the desire to do it? I no longer felt that I needed to keep them updated about my life. I no longer needed their approval to make a change in my life.

The word "obligation" started fading away from my vocabulary.

I no longer felt like every Sunday had to be dedicated to phone calls with siblings. If I felt like sleeping in or staying in bed the whole day reading, resting and not talking to anyone, I did it without feeling guilty about it.

One of my siblings used to say, "No news, bad news." And that what I got them used to. When I needed some time off, it meant that I was at the bottom of a hole. And bottom of the hole I used to hit often.

I didn't understand how my body worked. I didn't understand that quiet time was good for me. If I was active I was fine, but as soon as I had some free time, I tried desperately to fill it. I would turn on the radio. I would call someone, sometimes while the radio was still on, and talk about nothing at all. I was afraid of the emptiness, I was afraid when everything was quiet. Afraid when I was alone with myself.

"What did you say? Alone with myself? Scary".

And scary it was.

I used to say,

"The times that I am not busy are exactly when I make bad decisions and get myself into trouble," and that was true.

There were evenings where I will be bored and alone, I didn't know what to do with myself.

One evening when I was feeling alone, I called a man who wanted to date me. I wasn't attractive enough to him to be in a relationship with him. He came over. And soon after the movie started, he wanted to cuddle. I became really annoyed. My boring evening was turning into an annoying evening, an evening I felt "forced" to spend with someone I didn't particularly like. I sat on the couch opposite to him and answered his questions with very short sentences.

"Would you like to go for a late dinner after the movie?"

"No, I feel tired," I said.

I became more and more annoyed, but I just couldn't bring myself to ask him to leave. I felt like the worst person ever that day. How can I take such advantage of a man who seems to like me? Now that he is here for me, how can I just ignore him?

It went on like that, me sitting on the opposite couch and him trying to have a conversation.

I eventually told him that I was feeling too tired and wanted to go to bed.

"So, thank you for coming, and I will talk to you later. Have a good night," I said before he even had a chance to believe that he was coming to bed with me.

The interesting part is that after he left, I felt more annoyed.

"Wasting my time with someone like that, what was I thinking? He wanted to sleep with me tonight, that's why he came to visit."

And that was my evening. A man wasn't able to free me from my boredom, but I was so annoyed that I never called him again.

"A man who doesn't know how to entertain me, what good is he?" I said to myself before getting comfortable and finishing the movie alone.

Obviously it was his fault, I thought. Before coming to my house, he should have known that he was coming just because I was bored, not because I wanted to sleep with him.

I fell asleep feeling bored. The movie didn't help.

Eventually I had to stop and look at myself in the mirror, smile to myself and say, "I love you, I like spending time with you."

It took time for me to accept myself and enjoy every minute I spend with myself.

Often, this question goes through my mind:

"Who do you think you are fooling? You don't love who you are, saying it will not change anything."

But it actually changed a lot. I went from barely being able to look at myself in the mirror and say "I love you" to actually looking myself in the eyes, posing, saying, "I love you Mabelle," and then taking few deep breaths to let the words sink in. I smile at myself in the mirror anytime I walk past one, and if I have more time, I let myself know how beautiful I am and what an incredible woman I am.

Now, I often find myself laughing—not at myself, but with love and compassion toward myself.

Not only did that exercise allow me to love what I was seeing in the mirror, but also to fully allow myself to relax. I have learned to sit and just enjoy a quiet moment, either reading or lying down and doing nothing, just being. It calms my "itching feet." I no longer felt like I had to get out and always be doing something. I became less critical of who I am, my body shape, my skin complexion, and the freckles I have on my face. I disliked those freckles so much that I had a laser procedure to have them removed. The dermatologist removed several, but they kept coming back. I found myself with more freckles than I had before. Like they say in French:

"Chassez le naturel et il revient au galop." What's bred in the bone will come out in the flesh.

I had to learn to relax and accept the fact that I was doing nothing that needed to be done. Yes, there are dirty dishes in the sink, but they will still be there when I am done reading the chapter or finished a knitting round. Unless someone else did it for me, and then it would even be better.

Sundays are no longer my phone calls and cleaning day. I clean progressively throughout the week.

After an evening supper, I have a friend who asked me, "What would you do if someone kidnapped you, took you away and put you in a dark cell without any explanation you? What would you do?"

That will mean I would be alone with myself. Since I wouldn't know what was happening or where I was, I could let my mind make up a whole scenario, try to imagine what I did that put me in that situation and make a scary movie out of it. Or I could just sit back, calm down and meditate, rest, and sleep.

But the real question is:

How effective is my ability to think clearly when I am afraid?

When I am afraid, my ability to think clearly is reduced. My thoughts are focused on how I can get out of the situation, and that means that I forget to pay attention to what is causing the feeling. I spend all my energy trying to find an escape from the situation. This often creates more trouble in my

Life, and I dig myself a pretty deep hole. The fear stays with me longer, because it is all I think about.

I often find that when I am asked, "What do you do?" I answer, "I am an electrician" or "I am in school" or "I am working for this company." These answers show that I define myself as my job and my school.

But the answer to the question "What do you do?" can go further, I hope that is not all I am doing on earth.

I work, but that doesn't define who I am.

-What defines me then?

It took me years to be able to answer that question. Yes, I am a soul in a body experiencing a journey on the planet earth, but is that all?

I am defined by: my big heart; my compassion toward myself and other beings; my happy and contagious spirit; my down times; my moments of feeling depressed; my moments of reaching out to others to seek comfort and love; my moments of sharing love; and my time spent supporting and helping family members, friends and strangers.

I am an amazing being. I am complex, but yet simple. I have moments of anger and disappointment, of crying out loud, of screaming, being upset and being jealous. I have moments of laughter's, moments of sharing, moments of simply loving this amazing being that I am.

All of those feelings make me who I am. Recognizing those feelings without attachment make me who I am.

I am co-creator

_____

_____

_____

_____

_____

_____

_____

_____

_____

_____

_____

_____

_____

_____

_____

_____

_____

_____

_____

_____

_____

_____

_____

_____

_____

_____

_____

_____

_____

_____

_____

_____

_____

_____

_____

_____

_____

_____

_____

_____

_____

_____

I am co-creator

_____

_____

_____

_____

_____

_____

_____

_____

_____

_____

_____

_____

_____

_____

_____

_____

_____

_____

_____

_____

_____

Chapter Six

Intentions

"My daily meditation routine"
"No one criticizes me; they point out
my talents, my qualities"
"How I see the world is what lies deep within me"
"The pain is telling me to stop and to
take care of my physical body"
"I am the best friend anyone could wish to have"

I came to realize that LIFE, living is all about intentions, daily intentions.

I have always had the intention to be healthy, wealthy and happy.

In 2014, I had few health issues. I hit rock bottom. I stayed at a job I didn't like for over a year. Working in a different town, away from home. The original plan was to work at that job for six months, save some money and move on. A year later, I was still getting up at 4:30 in the morning, catching up the bus at 5:30 to go to a job I didn't like and still not being able to save any money.

Until that point in my life, I had reasons for working hard: buying a house and going back to school at the same time; sending money to family members, a trip to Europe; saving for a safari in Kenya or a trip to Central America. I had been able to justify working in a profession I didn't enjoy. I was able to put aside envisioning what I really wanted to become.

I learned at a young age to be thankful for what I have, to be content, to not ask for better or more. I was taught to be thankful. At least I was working, making money. I had food on the table, money in my pocket and was able to pay all the bills. I had no reason to complain. I was living a life that fulfilled what was expected of me.

Travelling became my big motivator, and it was great.

But working that job, I had to ask myself deeper questions: "What was I missing in my life?" "How come I wasn't able to save any money?" The job paid well.

For months, every morning I asked myself if that day should be my last. I asked myself if it was a good day to take my own life. But I thought of the people I would leave behind. I knew the impact it would have on my family, my siblings, and my mother. I was a spiritual guide to my niece, who was dealing at the time with some personnel issues. My sisters who was my best friend. My soul sister, with whom I had a deep connection. They would be devastated. I couldn't begin to bring myself to imagine the impact it would have on the man who was sharing my life. I thought of my garden blooming in the spring. Leaving it made me feel guilty. The guilt would take me right out of my head and into my heart. I would realize that it wasn't all about me, and I would drag my shell out of bed. I was empty, but up and ready for another day at a job I didn't like, trying to hold on until the evening. I started gaining weight despite the fact that I was eating healthy and was physically active.

And I had always intended to be happy and healthy.

Financially, I was digging myself into debt. No matter how much I paid back into the credit card, I was never able to pay it down.

During these tense periods of my life, I couldn't understand why I wasn't bringing forward the health and wealth I fully intended. I let stress push me away from my daily meditation, my five-minute morning yoga and the long walks.

And it finally hit me: I was way too focused on what I didn't want. By checking my bank account several times a day, I was demonstrating a fear of lack. I needed to make sure, every day, many times a day, that there was enough money in my bank account to pay the bills. Even if I wasn't paying any bills that day, I was in fear of the coming bills. It became clear that I needed to change careers, that travelling should not be an escape, but a pleasure. However, I ignored these insights and continued to live the old way. Physical ailments are the last signal from my body telling me that something is not going right in my life. And I had physical ailments. I found myself in the emergency room one evening with chest pain. My knees were so inflamed that I had to give up hiking, running, yoga and even long walks. I would have difficulty getting up after I squatted, I often needed help or a support to pry myself up.

My moral was as low as it had ever been. Unfortunately it wasn't a short period of time. This period lasted over two years. The doctors tried to convince me that I was depressed and needed to be on pills. I fled from those doctors. I had meaning in life. I wasn't isolated. I loved my family and spent hours on the phone with them. I had a great supportive circle of friends. I felt like I was stuck, not depressed. None of the doctors seemed interested in supporting, guiding people out of being stuck. I turned to psychologists. I soon found myself repeating myself at almost every session. I was getting nowhere and spending money. I gave up on the doctors and psychologists.

What do I do when I feel stuck? Who do I see?

I had no idea where to even begin. Online research didn't help.

I was pushing my boyfriend away by being in a terrible mood daily. I was lying to my friends, pushing them away by making excuses to not see them. Most of all, I was no longer happy. I started disliking who I was becoming.

I read self-development books ferociously. What was I doing with my life? Where was I going? What was my purpose in life? I became more and more confused.

I needed to return to my Intentions: be healthy, happy and wealthy. I had none of those in my life. So, what was I doing wrong? Or what was I not doing?

I no longer meditated. I knew daily meditation created happiness within, helped me have a quieter mind. I knew it helped me trust my intuitions because I was able to quiet the chattering in my head. Meditation allowed me to understand the difference between being afraid and just being cautious.

After many failed starts, I stopped trying on my own and went to a ten-day silent meditation retreat. I didn't want any distractions. I was looking for quiet and peace of mind. I am a chatty person, and I often felt like my mission was to save people. I needed to be silent for ten days. I realized the benefit of the meditation after the third day. But the first three days were a nightmare. I would come up with any excuse to quit:

I need to call home to make sure that my boyfriend is doing well.

I need to check my voicemail just in case there is an emergency.

I am getting by well enough. My co-workers are the one who need to be at this retreat, not me.

But I was there because I didn't want to just "get by." I wanted to Live Intentionally Fully Eternally. Actually, shame made me stay for The last 7 days. I was way too embarrassed to leave while other people stayed. I also knew that I would be kicking myself in the derriere if I left. So I stayed. I stayed for ten days, ten days of daily meditation. I slept, meditated, ate, walked, meditated, snacked, meditated, ate, meditated, and repeated it all over again for the next nine days. The silence allowed me not to rush to help someone who was crying or having a difficult time. I didn't feel like I had to always be happy and smile at everyone even when

I was feeling down. It was the first step toward observing and accepting my emotions.

After the retreat, I was able to restart my daily meditation routine. Some days, it was just five minutes before falling asleep, but I did it.

I changed my attitude toward the pain I was feeling in my knees. Instead of focusing on all the activities I could no longer do, I rubbed them and told them how much I loved them and understood they were just trying to get my attention. The pain was their way of telling me to stop and take care of my physical body. Slowly, I started integrating short walks and hikes into my life. I stopped when I felt any discomfort in my knees. Instead of pushing myself and becoming angry that I could not finish, I stopped before the timer went off. I started running one minute at a time. Yes, it was frustrating to be out of breath after a ten minute run, but I knew I needed to begin slowly to take care of my knees and my physical health. I felt grateful for the time I was in better shape and could run for a longer period time and not be out of breath. I truly found out that I used to be in shape when I found myself out of shape and had to start all over again. I have always taken being in good physical condition for granted.

"What is my purpose?"

What if my purpose was TO BE? Just TO BE? When I AM, when I AM present, everything falls into place. The universe works for and with me, for my wellbeing and my growth. When I AM, I love myself. Only by loving myself, I can tap into the energy of co-creation. Only by loving myself can I do what is profitable for my growth. Only by loving myself can I use and share my talents.

Being raised Jehovah's Witness, the Bible was part of my life. It was a subject of pride for my mum because I could read the Bible before Grade One. One of the games we often played when I was a kid was to recite all the books of the Bible, in order, without looking. We never had a reward for the winner, knowing all the books of the Bible was a reward on its own. I gave my first public speech in church when I was eight years old. Through reading the bible, I learned that I needed to love myself first: "You shall love your neighbour as yourself" (Romans 13:9b)* If I don't love myself, how can I love my neighbours? I cannot offer what

I don't have or don't know I have. What I project into the world is what lies deep within me.

When I get to the point where I am comfortable with myself, where I love myself enough to create a loving world around me, I can freely and easily tap into the talents I have within me. My talents are looking to be expressed not suppressed. For many years, I believed I didn't have any talent. I had a friend, a gentle sweet lady I met when I first moved to Canada. She was a volunteer at a program that pairs a Canadian with a newcomer. I was the newcomer, she was the warm heart that would support and guide me. She was my guide, a friend I could rely on so that I was not alone in a new country. She took me shopping for winter clothing. She took me to different malls and even gave me a Christmas gift before leaving the town to go spend the holidays with her family. She spoke fluent Spanish, English, and French. During the summer, she decided to volunteer in Brazil. She began learning Portuguese to the point of being fluent when she got back from Brazil. I moved to another province, and she moved to another country. In Germany, she started learning German.

Besides being fluent in many languages, she played the guitar and had a musical ear. I eventually bought a guitar, I played it many time without tuning it, because I just couldn't hear the notes. She would tune it for me when she visited me and advised me to buy a tuner. Above all, she had a big heart.

I admired her and envied her at the same time. "How can someone be so talented?" Not only was she talented already, she kept learning more and more skills.

The parable of Talents in the book of Matthew tells the story of a master who had to travel to another kingdom. Before leaving, he called in his servants and gives them gifts. "To one, he gave five talents, to another two, and to another one." When he returned from his long journey, he called all the servants to whom he gave the gifts and asked for a report. "One who received five talents came and brought five more talents. He who had received two talents came and said 'I have gained two more talents'." The servant who received one talent from the master said, "I was afraid and went and hid your talent in the ground." The master took the talent from the one that hid his talent.

The parable makes me laugh because how many times did I envy people who had several talents and kept creating more and more talents. "Besides singing, you are an excellent dancer, and you play multiple instruments? You draw as well? Oh, and you speak eight languages fluently? Is that all? No, you run marathons. You teach yoga and volunteer around the world? Ok, it was nice talking to you." But while I am envying that person, I forget that I have talents too. They might not be the same as the person talking to me, but they are talents.

"What do I do with my talent?"

The master didn't feel sorry for the servant who did nothing with his talent. Instead, he took the talent away. I don't want to lose my talent. So I might as well do something with it. But, what are my talents?

I began using a technique to find my talents. I listened to others when they give me a compliment. I stopped asking myself if they mean it or not because that doesn't matter.

When someone said, "Your laugh is contagious", I heard "You have a laugh that heals."

When someone said, "You give incredible hugs", I heard "You are a warm being."

When someone said, "I feel so cared for", I heard "You are the best friend anyone could wish to have."

Even when someone said, "Esther you are annoying, always paying attention to any small details", I heard "You are a well-organized person."

"You always want a clean house and everything in a specific place", I heard "You have a clear mind. You don't like clutter, and your time is precious."

No one criticizes me, they point my talents, my qualities.

I stopped playing the guitar many years ago, because it required more effort and commitment from someone like me who does not have musical talents. It doesn't mean that I cannot play guitar or any other musical instrument, it just means that I need to spend more time practicing than one who is musically talented. I can learn to be patient, and maybe by doing so, I can develop a new talent along with playing a musical instrument, PATIENCE. Maybe, even one day, I will be able to sing and love what I hear.

Maybe LIFE gave me one talent, and if I use it, I can create many more talents before I depart this physical world.

I am co-creator

_____

_____

_____

_____

_____

_____

_____

_____

_____

_____

_____

_____

_____

_____

_____

_____

_____

_____

_____

I am co-creator

_____

_____

_____

_____

_____

_____

_____

_____

_____

_____

_____

_____

_____

_____

_____

_____

_____

_____

_____

_____

_____

Chapter Seven

Beliefs

*"With love I let my family members
learn at their own pace"*
"He never told me he loved me, but I know he did"
"As an adult I can have my own beliefs,
"Practice becomes a habit; habit becomes LIFE"

Driving home one day, I noticed that the car ahead of me had a flat tire on the back driver's side. As soon as I saw it, my mission was to let the driver know. I had a goal, a purpose. I drove closer to him asking myself these questions:

"Does he know that the tire is flat? Can he feel the car vibrating differently?"

He came to a stop at a stop sign on a quiet road, and I pulled beside him with smile on my face, the Mother Teresa vibrating in me. The angels were telling me, "You can do it. We are so proud of you." The cheerleaders in heaven, if there are such things, were jumping up and down for me, performing acrobatics that I had never seen before.

I waited for him to look in my direction. When he did, I pointed to the flat tire on the rear of his car.

"Yes I did it! I, maybe, just saved someone," I thought.

My head swelled, full of pride. "You did it, Esther. You did it."

His reaction was unexpected. He was mad, really mad. His had a stern look on his face. He made a gesture that was very far from a thank you and looked away. Then he pulled forward and made the turn. I was deflated. My head shrunk. The cheerleaders were no longer dancing. My shoulders slumped, and my halo clattered to the floor.

A honk brought me back, and I remembered I still had to drive. I slowly pulled ahead and turned.

I immediately began to feel sorry for myself:

"Poor me, maybe I need to find this man; where is his car? I needed to explain myself, let him know that I wasn't going to cut him off. I had to tell him that I wanted to help, to give him a hand, explain that he needed to pump air in that tire. Poor, poor me."

-*"So, what's the problem?"*

-"The problem is that my objective was to help, and I got the opposite reaction. The man didn't understand me. No one understands me"

-*"Ok, so, what's the problem?"*

-"I just told you, the man—"

-"*I heard you, but you are just telling me what happened. What's the problem? What's making you feel so distressed?*"

Really? Do I have to repeat myself again?

-"So like I was saying, the man—"

-"*These are just facts, Esther. You are telling me what happened, and I know what happened. I am your guide, I know. The question is: What bugs you about his reaction? He has the right to react the way he chooses to. What about you, what's the problem?*"

Let me tell you more about this voice. A few years ago, I noticed that she wasn't just a constant nagging voice, but an incredible guide, an ally who answers my questions when I ask them. However, most of the time, she does not give the answer I expected. There were times when I didn't listen. I knew myself better. Who was she to tell me otherwise? I could follow my human way of reasoning and have the result I want, and even though I might hit my head against the wall many times, at one point, I will get what I want. I learned, sometimes the hard way, but I learned. Now I pay more attention to what she says, and I keep her busy. She has become my friend, my confident. When a situation arises, and I am so confused that I cannot even see the tip of my nose, I stop and ask her, "So now what? What do I do?" Those questions help my head to clear up and I wait, the answer always comes, she always answers me.

A few years ago, I felt out of place living in Quebec, I felt like it wasn't my place to be. Yes, I was an immigrant, a new immigrant, but it seems like there was no door open big enough for me to go through. I could not find a full time job despite the fact that I was ready to do any job. My last summer in Quebec, not knowing that it was my last summer in that beautiful province, I got hired as a sport attendant for a hotel in a town I have never heard of. Part of the contract was to stay and live in the hotel for the entire summer. I packed my luggage and moved to the small town of Val-David and lived an amazing experience, one of my best summer at the time. I still knew that I needed to move to a new town or province. I knew that that job was just temporary; September will soon come and I will have to go back to Montreal and hope for a full time job.

But, do I have to go back to Montreal? Do I have to spend another winter in Montreal? I then felt compelled to move to a new province, a new town, away from my family.

Not having enough money saved, I took a bus and spent fifty-two hours on the trip. I arrived at a hostel in Edmonton five pounds lighter because I didn't want to spent any of the money I had to eat; I slept most of the way and spent $3 on a sandwich the second day of the trip.

Being alone in a new province, a new town and not being able to speak the language, I started paying closer attention to that voice in my head. While looking online to find a room for rent with an immediate moving date, I found myself on a website I didn't search for and found the perfect room not only with an amazing owner, but in a great community as well. It is her who guided me in finding it. Since then, our conversations have become more frequent and more distinct.

But now, I was in a different state of mind. I just wanted to cry and complain about that man who misread my intentions. I wanted to have her on my side. I wanted her to agree with the way I was feeling.

And here she was, not on my side at all. A true guide is someone who will say, "Poor Mabelle, my poor beloved, this guy did wrong to you! How terrible that was. You just wanted to help!" But, no! And since I welcomed her in my life, acknowledged her in my life, and in my life she has always been, it is hard to ignore her.

I did try to ignore her, hoping she would tire and go away.

-*"So what bugs you about this man's reaction?"*

If my guide didn't even feel sorry for me, who would? I answered, hoping she would leave me alone.

-"No one understands me. I was performing a good deed. People always misunderstand me and interpret what I am doing the wrong way."

-*"And for those people whom you say misunderstand you, does explaining yourself help?"*

-"Rarely."

-*"So is it important for you to explain yourself?"*

-"No, I don't care. They can think what they want about me."

-"*So what in that man's reaction, a man you never met before and might never meet again, affect you so much?*"

Like I said, she is a smart guide.

-"It just reminded me of all of those times where my actions, words, were weighed and judged. It just reminded me that no one cares."

-"*You know by now that we choose to believe in someone or something, that we choose to let a message touch us or not, that we cannot control the reactions of others, that we can only work on ourselves, on how we react in Life.*

If someone's action bugs you, the question is not 'How dare he does that to me?' but, instead, observe and ask yourself:

'Hey, what is that emotion coming up?' Identify the emotion without judgment, acknowledge it. Say to yourself, 'I've noticed you, and thank you for showing up. I also thank the person who helped bring that emotion forth. Now I can work on it and release it.'

It doesn't matter how far in your LIFE those emotions go to, when they originated first or who instigated them in you, what matter is that they are resurfacing and looking for your attention.

Just do a cleanse by releasing them; tell them, 'I thank you for showing up, for reminding me that I need to put that luggage down and continue on my path. I release you and release all the negative emotions connected to this event.' Then, take a few deep breaths and carry on your day"

Is it that easy? I asked myself. As a human, I was expecting something harder, more involving.

But when I am in the moment, it becomes hard to remember that advice. But when I eventually remember, I stop and do the cleanse. I then release those emotions without blaming myself because I let them bother my conscience in the first place.

Practice becomes a habit, habit becomes LIFE. When I have the opportunity, I practice letting go of emotions that no longer serve any purpose in my life.

I bless them, there are no bad emotions. There are just emotions. There are no bad or good events, there are just events. I, myself choose to add the good or bad to any emotion or event.

When my sister married, I thought it was a *bad* event. She was so young, and I thought she had so much possibility ahead of her. She thought it was a great event. She was happy, she was in love.

If someone believes that they are unhappy even though they have five kids, three grandkids, and two great grandkids, and spend the weekend with their family, who am I to tell them that they should be grateful? Yes, I can mention it, but they don't have to see it the way I see it, because they choose to feel the way they feel. That person is not me, and that person's life is NOT MY EXPERIENCE. I choose whether or not to listen to their complaints. And I choose not to listen to it.

I can try to drill a belief into a kid's head; but when she becomes an adult, it is up to her to choose her own path.

I could be mad at her because she chose a different path, but that will certainly create tension between us and spoil a cherished relationship. Or I could accept it. And when I am asked for advice, give advice. It will always be up to her to decide to apply it.

When I was a child, my dad, Mr. Nutritious, always had something healthy to add to our supper salad. For many years, there was always green cabbage in the salad with other seeds and vegetables. I couldn't stand the taste of the green cabbage, but I had no other choice that to eat it; it was part of the salad, and there was not "picking out what you don't like Mabelle" allowed at the dinner table. I had to eat the salad as it was.

In quest of always finding something more nutritious, better for our health, one evening I was introduced to the red cabbage in the salad. Mr. Nutritious has discovered the red cabbage! Did I eat it? Yes I did, sometimes. One evening we were eating outside. The outdoor dining table was put in the big beach sand area my dad made for us kids to play in. I would take a mouth full of that "deliciously" filled salad with red cabbage salad, look around, dig a hole in the sand with my foot and spit the whole content of my mouth in the hole while no one was looking. I did that for the entire salad.

I am glad my father's red cabbage phase didn't last long and we were back eating our regular salad with grains.

Yes, cabbage is nutritious. It contains several vitamins. But as a kid, I hated eating that red cabbage. I had to eat it. It was the starter and to have dinner I had to finish my plate of salad

Was it because of the color or my belief that it had a strong taste?

I had to eat that cabbage when I was home. To this day, I still don't like eating cabbage; I will have it as juice mixed with many other fruits and vegetables to the point that I can't taste it. All of those years of being forced to eat cabbage at home didn't make me like the taste, didn't change my first feeling toward cabbage.

My dad provided us the food he believed that was nutritious for us, even if I didn't like it. Now as an adult I choose to acknowledge the nutritious properties of the cabbage, and stay as much as possible away from it. I eat other nutritious food that I like and I am fine.

As kid, I followed my parents, my dad's beliefs. As an adult, I can have my own beliefs, ones that suit me better, the ones that allow me to grow and to be happy and healthy.

I am co-creator

_____

_____

_____

_____

_____

_____

_____

_____

_____

_____

_____

_____

_____

_____

_____

_____

_____

_____

_____

_____

I am co-creator

_____

_____

_____

_____

_____

_____

_____

_____

_____

_____

_____

_____

_____

_____

_____

_____

_____

_____

_____

_____

_____

_____

Chapter Eight

I Am Co-Creator

"I spend my energy on the solution"
"One day at the time, this is my goal"
"I choose my life to be filled with Joy, Love,
Happiness and Abundance. And Voila"
"I shift my attention and my intentions shift"

In Genesis, the book that describes step by step the beginning of the creation, it is said

"God said 'Let us make humankind in our image, according to our likeness' So God created mankind in his own image, in the image of God he created them"

God created man in his image, which means that I have a part of me which is God. Therefore, if God has created me in his image, God has definitely given me the resources to be happy.

Very often I find myself caught in this scheme of turning outwards to be happy, to be loved, and I realize that each time that person went, that the situation ended, the job was over, my world collapsed with it.

While in prayer I asked myself, or rather I asked: "How can I be happy inside? How can I have peace within?"

Here are the answers, rather the answer I received

"LOVE YOURSELF".

Is that so simple?

Being who I am, I was expecting something more complicated because if it is not complicated it meant that it wouldn't work.

"But I love myself" I've answered

"In this case, you will not need external situation in order to be proven that you are lovable".

Damn, I got caught with my hand in the bag.

So I started a path of "meeting the creature created by God in his image." I paid more attention to my thoughts, my reactions to situations I've faced. I realized that I loved to play the victim, but in a subtle way, just tell a story, keep quiet and let others feel sorry for me.

I realized that I have often thought about situation I didn't want to manifest in my life,

"Oh no, I will not miss my bus again"

"I'm sure I'll get hired by a company which doesn't respect women... ".

I often used words like always, never.

I NEVER had enough money.

I ALWAYS got hired for jobs I did not like.

Then I would spend my day making a movie of victim, of "poor me" in my head. "Just smile to

everyone and think in your head 'how can't they see that I am unhappy?' And blame them.

It is SUPER HYPER exhausting to live life like that, to think that other "outside" do not understand me and keep it all inside.

To think that I am not worthy, so even if a good situation presents itself, go without paying attention to it, busy as I was at seeing life as an horror movie.

It's like an addiction; an alcoholic needs his daily dose of alcohol to feel "good". So I needed my daily dose of self-pity to feel "good".

The truth is that I was not happy, not at all, I had friends, I hung on to them like a safety belt, a shouting voice very low

"Please save me, save me, I am that little unfortunate girl".

It has led me to have no barrier.

"You can take advantage of me as much as you want as long as you pretend to love me".

And I had friends who took advantage of it without me interfering, and hey it's me who open my door to them. I was pretending, I thought that I was "lying to others," but what I realized is that

I have to lie to myself first before even lying to someone else, and it is a bit of self-destruction.

I stopped and observed. Who is wearing my boots? Yes who is living my life?

"ME, ME, ME".

So I am responsible for my life?

"YES, YES, YES".

If I was created in God's image, that means I am a part of God, that means, I am god and therefore creator of my life. So I decided to "take things in hand," be creator.

I decided that any thought, any action I will take on my part will be thought or taken consciously, instead of "you make me angry" it will be "I am allowing myself to be angry and I am putting in anger".

Therefor I am fully conscious in that anger. By doing so I am taking power away from that feeling of anger and I am not allowing this anger to dictate my action.

Love myself means not to "hit me" when I miss some opportunities, it is to say "Oops that is unfortunate my beautiful, next time," and when I'm not fast enough and I "hit myself with

non-constructive words" of which I am aware, I apologize and tell me how much I loved myself and that I am doing the best I know at the moment. This is the activity I practice often, telling myself that I love me, telling the situation I encountered that I love it and everyone involved in that situation.

Recently I didn't work for a year, I went back to school, and when it was time to get back on the job force, work wasn't happening as fast as I wanted. At first, I was frustrated. I was ready to go back to work, but it felt like no companies were hiring or that I wasn't qualified enough for the ones that were hiring. My frustration got to the point that all I was thinking of the whole day was about FINDING a job.

I stopped and I decided, chose to take one day at the time and be present in every day of my life, and take each day as it comes.

I remembered this verse of the bible where Jesus spoke of birds:

"Look at the birds of the sky, they don't sow nor reap nor gather into stores, yet your Heavenly Father feeds them... doesn't the soul need more than food and the body more than the clothing?...

Which one of you by worrying can add one cubit to his life."

If, and I was created in the image of God, that same God who made the birds and the lilies of the field, and takes care of them, he will take care of me also; birds live one day at the time time, the flowers also, tomorrow may never come.

One day at the time, this was my goal, and every day I had "bread on my plate, water on my table and money to buy what I needed that day". When I found myself "financially stuck", someone offered to lend me some money, or just gave it to me, odd jobs appeared. My thoughts were of daily thoughts of "my needs are taken care of", with no doubt. I did not spend one second on the "problem" because problem there is not, there is just a step, step I needed to take either with a positive attitude, then everything goes well, enjoy my months at home to finish a good portion of the basement, or with a negative attitude which I refuse to experiment.

Spend time on the so-called problem only give it my full attention. I've already seen children who need attention, after 5 minutes it is painful: "hey look at me, I jump, I just hurts myself, look at me"

oh well, it is like a "problem", if I give it my full attention it will become bigger and bigger to the point where I am no longer able to even see the path I am walking on.

There is a problem, though, "I have no money to pay the mortgage this month?" Well, what do I want? Pay the mortgage of course, well, then I spend my energy on the solution.

If there is a child who has bad grades in math, and all I do is talk to him about those bad grades, his grade will not improve unless I help him with the subject he is having difficulties understanding. if I do not address how to help him have better grade, it will not improve, it will only the day we come together with a way that works for him, and it is pointless to even start helping him if I think that it will not work.

For the job, I knew exactly what I wanted, the kind of company I wanted to work for; I had a job offer that I refused, not interested to work outside of the city, I like to sleep in my bed every night, unless I am out and about again-as-always. Knowing that it was almost the end of the month and the mortgage needed to be paid, I asked for

some money, I did not have the money to pay; work one day "appeared", I discovered that I had a pension fund somewhere, paid by my last employer that I could withdraw whenever I wanted..

After some time, I was hired by a company that met the criteria I was looking for in a company.

If I am and I am the co creator of my life, so I chose my life to be filled with joy, happiness, love and abundance, and VOILA.

Low moments? I practice Ho'Oponopono : "I'm sorry, please forgive me, I love you, thank you," I take an inspirational book that I read, sleep making myself happy movies at time where my mind will just not turn off, because my mind will make its own movies anyway, go for a walk, to the gym, or call a friend, empty a little bit the stories that might be going on in my head. Quiet that small-to protective voice in my head.

Here is a piece of my journey. I love you.

WHAT I THINK OR SAY I BECOME.

I am co-creator

_____

_____

_____

_____

_____

_____

_____

_____

_____

_____

_____

_____

_____

_____

_____

_____

_____

_____

_____

_____

_____

_____

_____

_____

_____

_____

_____

_____

_____

_____

_____

_____

_____

_____

_____

_____

_____

_____

_____

_____

_____

_____

_____

I am co-creator

_____

_____

_____

_____

_____

_____

_____

_____

_____

_____

_____

_____

_____

_____

_____

_____

_____

_____

_____

_____

_____

Chapter Nine

My Past

"Experiences arise in life so I can learn from them"
"Who am I to want to change her?"
*"I did exactly what I knew at the
time; now let move on"*
"It is for me to open my heart"

How do I react when I face a frightening situation? An unpleasant situation?

Do I sometimes find myself giving power to someone, letting a past situation dictate my choices today?

I was going to school in a different town. On a nice evening at home, after pizza and couple glasses of wine, I started thinking of my dad. I often think about him, but this time it was different. I realized, after over seventeen years that he was gone for real. I could no longer see him as a physical being. That emotion was intense. I was thrown in. It felt like I had just received the call telling me that he had passed away. Even though it happened 17 years ago, it felt present. I was not able to convince myself that it had already happened. My brain, my whole body was thrown into sadness. I swam into it.

It brought back memories, happy memories of time spent with my dad. They were memories I didn't want to bring up, because they meant I would never again have those times with my dad. I remember his Sunday lunch. Sundays were his days to cook.

Even though it had been seventeen years, I begged him not to die, to stay with us. I found myself a teenager again, a girl who didn't want her dad to die and was refusing to face the fact that it has already happened.

I sat on my bed, in the small bedroom I was renting and cried. Cried, doing my best to not ask why, to just let the feeling be, let the tears flush the sadness out of my body. For a moment, I was so deep into the sadness that I could no longer feel parts of my body. I could no longer feel my buttocks sitting on the bed or my hands covering my eyes that were soaked with tears. I was in the room, but at the same time I was in my pain, my sadness. I felt the sadness take over every single part of my body, flow through my veins and become me. I felt such a deep pain. I don't know how long it lasted, but at one point, I had a moment of clarity, I just relaxed, breathed through the tears, and accepted them without judging myself.

I started laughing. It was a true laugh, a laugh within me without anything exterior provoking it. I gently laughed at myself for being silly. Silly?

"What are those memories about? What am I crying about?" I asked myself.

They were unfulfilled expectations, unfulfilled hope and desires. Yes, I missed my dad, but I mostly missed the moments we would not spend together, the time I expected us to have together. I don't literally miss not having him around, but I miss not spending time with him. I wish that my father could have told me more about his life, his childhood, his parents and siblings, so I would know where I come from. He passed away when I was so young; I didn't have the chance to ask him about his mother, my grandma, whom I have never met.

After his passing, I hoped that my mother would love me the way I needed to be loved. I hoped she would fill up the emptiness in my heart, love me the way I wanted her to love me, and teach me about life in a way that I could understand while protecting me so that I never hurt myself or had a broken heart. When my mother couldn't fill those needs, I looked for a man in my life that could give me what I didn't have from my mum.

Sitting on the bed, I realized I was crying over memories that never happened, situations that could have, should have, or might have happened according to a movie I had imagined. I laughed and laughed harder. How could I feel pain or resentment about something that doesn't exist and never did?

I realized that my mind was so strong and powerful that it could bring to the present, right now, right here, a situation that never happened and make it so real!

I was feeling sad, worrying about, nothing. Nothing happened, a lot of things could have happened, but none of them did. What happened was my dad passed away seventeen years ago. How could I know what situation would have been good for me? How do I know that in being loved differently by my parents, my life would have been better today? Better compared to what? Yes, compared to what? Compared to the person who looks happy all the time and seems to always be on a fluffy cloud? What do I know about that person and their life experiences? Nothing.

My mother is a warm welcoming person. She will always make her guests feel at home.

I remember when I was still living at home, her house was a place for singles, people who lived alone. They were family acquaintances and close family friends who will come visit and stay over lunch and supper. She always fed her guests, sometimes even before her own children. When it was time for the guest to leave, she would give them enough money for the fare plus extra in case they need to get something on their way home.

Still, with all of her generosity toward her guests, all the meals cooked with love every day for all of her children, I still didn't feel loved.

I often thought that she probably cooked, fed, and dressed me because she was worried about what people would say if they saw one of her kids wandering around unfed and not properly dressed. I used that reasoning to convince myself that she never loved me. If anyone pointed out her love was in all of the things she did for me, I'd say she didn't have any choice.

My mother would often say to me, "You are lazy. You are just a lazy girl. No man will ever want to marry a lazy girl like you. You never help around the house. You're sitting there watching me clean the house. Come and help me you lazy girl." I heard the word "lazy" so many times that I thought it had to be my middle name. I figured that doing the dishes once a week, then once a month was enough, because that was what she deserved for not spending any time with me.

Now, I realized that my mother's needed me to show her love by helping her with the house chores. I never felt like I needed to help around the house. I would when I was in the mood, which was almost never. When my mother divided the duties, mine was to wash the dishes and my little sister was to clean the living room. I did my duty for a couple of weeks and decided that I no longer needed to do the dishes, because I proved to her that I knew how to do the dishes. I always answered her sharply anytime she asked me to help her, "Don't worry, when I have my own house, it will be clean and spotless."

If all she needed to feel loved was me helping her around the house, I can't imagine how frustrated she could have been when she looked at me not helping at all. No wonder that she spoke to me in what I thought was an unloving way.

All I was craving for was for her to spend time with me, one-on-one, but unfortunately those moments were only when she came to my bedroom early in the morning, before anyone was up to tell me about what I wasn't doing right.

I could have improved my understanding of what she was looking for to feel loved by me, instead of doing exactly the opposite of what she needed to feel loved and appreciated, so she could speak to me in a loving way.

What prevented me from doing so?

I did exactly what I knew at the time, reacted the only way I knew how to react toward her.

On a certain level, I needed this situation to feed my own self-pity. I did exactly what I knew, and I bet she did exactly what she knew. I realize now that if I find myself blaming her for acting the way she did toward me, the only way she knew how to, then I should also blame myself as well for acting the way I did toward her.

Honestly, what is the fun in blaming myself or my mother? What am I getting for constantly blaming her or myself? Absolutely nothing. I get nothing constructive that helps me grow and become a better person completely responsible of her own actions and decisions. She learns her way at her rhythm, I learn my way at my own rhythm. Loving her means fully accepting her as she is and respecting her limitations and her learning process.

One summer day, I was driving to meet a couple of friends to hike and camp in the mountains. Even though I didn't enjoy camping, I let myself be convinced to try it again. So there I was, driving to meet my friends, listening to the radio when my phone rang. I assumed my friends were calling to see when I would arrive. But the voice on the phone was no other than my mum's. And for the first time in twenty-nine years on this planet, I was happy to hear her voice.

"Hey it's you, how are you?" I said with the smile in my voice.

The fact that I didn't know she was calling prevented me from imagining the conversation we would have and thinking, "It's her again." The conversation went smoothly. I told her about my new job. She congratulated me. I told her about my weekend plans, and she told me how she was. Here we were, talking like two old friends. I never used to ask her about her life. It always led to something non-constructive. Eventually, I asked her to have my brother to call me. "You work now. You make money. We have no money, you call" she replied.

One second, two seconds, three seconds. A deep breath. Another deep breath. I stopped the voice that started in my mind. I stopped the scenario that was forming in my head. I took a deep breath. "Find something constructive to say. Come with a solution, not a plan for a battle," I told myself.

"Do you still have Internet home?" I asked.

"Yes," she replied.

"Ask him to call me via the Internet. It is free."

I gave her the time he could call me and hung up. I left the radio off, took several deep breaths. I smiled at myself. Told myself how proud of myself I was for not falling back into old patterns and for respecting mother and myself.

For years I said only the minimum in our conversations. They were as superficial as I could keep them without being rude to her. I had a blockage. I put up high my fences and refused to lower them for her. Any question about my private life felt like an invasion. As soon as I saw her number, I thought, "What does she want?" I transferred that energy into my voice and let that first thought dictate how the conversation went. The tone of my voice was unwelcoming on the phone because I was thinking about what I wanted to say before letting the words escape my mouth.

That day in the car, I was surprised, happily surprised, in the shift. We were able to have a great phone conversation with respect for each other. It was amazing what happened when I shifted my attitude, when I didn't project through my voice my feelings of not wanting to talk to her.

I thought I had built a thick skin, that her statements I perceived as being hurtful no longer affect me. I thought I had completely dealt with my belief of not being loved by her. I thought I had worked on it, and that I could feel nothing if she said something that was not constructive. And, then that conversation occurred to teach me to love her as she is. In any case do I want to change her, even if I could. It is her life, her path, and her journey, not mine. I accept her fully as she is. I can be mad, upset that she doesn't fulfill my expectations, or I can choose to be at peace with myself and accept who she is. Because the truth is I would not accept it if she tried to change me. And if I refuse to let her change me, who am I to want to change her?

"Do unto others what you want to be done unto you"

I refuse to let her change me, who am I to want to change her?

Those old patterns that were: "done with it, no longer affect me", and when I expect it the least, they come back, peers at the window of my life. Through the curtains, knock at the glass and with a big smile say:

"Hey, you remember me? I am your old friend; we had lot of fun together, do you remember those days we spent criticizing others that are not like us? I came to say hello, to see where you are at in your life, shake those old memories, let those memories make you cry, make you get upset and ruin your day; what do you think about that? Open the window, let me in. We had fun and we can have more fun. Or I have a better idea, open the doors, open them wide, let me shake those feelings, bring them back to the surface, bring those feelings from the past so you can feel them as there are happening now, take over how you feel today, because who cares about today? Let those emotions from the past guide

your LIFE TODAY and hang on to them. At least you know them, stay in your comfort zone, your safe zone. Do you remember when you used to feed yourself of me, and you had all those friends who will listen to you "cry" and tell them how you have never felt loved by your mum? Be the poor-me? You had lot of friends. Let me in and I will keep you in your comfort zone, a place that you are used to, because you've been there before, so you will know how to react, it will always be the same scenario, all will be the same. Let me in".

All that said with a nice charming smile. Attractive offer.

That day, it was my choice, either to let my old methods of handling relationships resurface and dictate my day, my life, or I could pull the curtain, turn the music up loud enough not to hear them, sing loud and terrible enough to make them run away, and choose, yes CHOOSE, how I want my day to be today. That is all I have, TODAY.

Experiences arise in life so I can learn from them and move forward, not so I can hang on to them, afraid to let them go. How can I learn if I am still hanging on to the old experiences and accepting only the old ways of doing things?

In grade school, there was something new to learn every year, to add to what was learned the previous year. In grade 1, I learned to recognize letters, numbers, write them down. I learned the difference between vowels and consonants. In grade 2, I added something new, counted up to a higher number, learned more complicated addition and subtraction. My writing improved. I tried different ways of holding my pen. My Grade 1 education helped me in my Grade 2. I didn't just hang on to what I learned in grade 1 and refuse to learn anything new in Grade 2. Imagine a seven-year-old telling the instructor, "Last year I learned my alphabet, consonants, vowels, I can write my name, read a bit, I think that is all I need in my life. I want to stay in that comfort zone." Of course that would lead to a parent-teacher meeting, me being in big trouble, and a well-deserved spanking from my parents.

In my journey on earth, there are no more parent-teacher meetings or spankings from mum or dad. Life spanks me. But, again, sometimes I need or deserve those spankings. I fully live the daily twenty-four hour gift I receive and am excited about it. Every day is a wrapped gift, a surprise. I want to know what is in that box and open it with excitement. That is how I choose to live every day, as a surprise, a gift.

I love travelling. I always enjoy my trips. I am so excited as soon as I plan a trip. I move toward the new. And when I return, I will let everyone know how great the trip was, what I have done. I hold no expectations when travelling, absolutely none. I am going on holidays, to a new country, I am excited, and I know it will be great. That's my attitude.

Shouldn't I apply that statement in my life? Shouldn't I choose to make every day a new beginning? Shouldn't I wake up in the morning and say, "I am starting a new day, a new beginning, how exciting!"

If someone comes to me with an issue that happened a day, week, month, decade ago, all I can do is to say "I am sorry". That takes place in the present, right now. I could try to go back to the past and undo the situation or try to erase that memory from the person's mind. I could try, but good luck. The truth is that the situation happened already. There is nothing I can do about it NOW. I can use the NOW and apologize for what happened and learn how to respond if a similar situation arises. I can go see a hypnotherapist and learn to forgive, move on, and live a different today than I did yesterday.

Do I need to learn from the past to create a better future and live a fuller present? What does it mean to learn from my past? Is it ensuring I do not make the same mistakes? While I am focusing on the mistakes I made in the past, aren't I going to create the same mistakes in my present life? What is the best way to look at my mistakes from my past? Is it true that I expand the emotions I focus on? Therefore, if I focus my attention on my past mistakes, wouldn't I, somehow create the same mistakes? That brings me to the question, "How can I create a better NOW, a NOW that I want without focusing my attention on my past?"

I believe that I possess within me the knowledge of comfort and discomfort. I am aware when I am not happy and feel uncomfortable. I know when something is wrong deep within me. I can ignore it or I can find a way to justify it to myself:

"My mum has always been sick, obviously I will always be sick as well" translates to, "I want to live exactly the life my mum lived. I am not responsible, my genes are."

"The doctor said I can never run again. I love running, but I can't ignore what the doctor said, after all he is a doctor" translates to, "I don't need to do anything. The doctor decides my fate. He is responsible for how I feel. I give him my power and he's responsible of telling me what I am able to do or not to do."

I want to TAKE the lesson from the "mistakes" I make in LIFE. I want to allow myself to experience LIFE on earth and when I feel sad, allow the sadness to be and to cry if needed.

I let go of a relationship few weeks before Christmas, and getting closer to Christmas time, I felt more and more anxious, I am going to spend Christmas alone in my house. I remember the previous Christmas spent with his family, the warmth of their house, the sharing, the hugs, the beautiful Christmas evening dinner by the fireplace and Christmas day breakfast, the unwrapping of the gifts. I found myself expecting this Christmas would be lonely and sad. Then I realized that there are infinite resources in the universe. It is for me to open my heart and welcome those resources in my life. I shifted my attention and my intentions. I blessed the previous Christmas, expressed my gratitude for living that experience. A couple of days before Christmas evening, a friend invited me for dinner with her family. I spent Christmas evening with good friends and ate a traditional Finnish Christmas dish. I even received Christmas gifts from her, her sister and other family friends. On Christmas day, another friend invited me to dinner with her family; I ate delicious Indian and Jamaican dishes and received a gift from her parents. There was a lot of laughter, sharing, and hugs at both celebrations.

I chose to leave my house and go to those two gatherings. I could have stayed home and cried about the Christmas I wasn't spending with my previous boyfriend's family. Saying YES to both invitations, leaving my house and going with an open heart, allowing myself to be part of the conversation, laugh at the jokes and give and receive hugs, made this Christmas a beautiful one, one of sharing, laughter, and unwrapping gifts.

Even though I missed them that Christmas, instead of dwelling on the past or what could have been, I decided to say YES to the offers and opportunities I had that day.

I am co-creator

_____

_____

_____

_____

_____

_____

_____

_____

_____

_____

_____

_____

_____

_____

_____

_____

_____

_____

_____

_____

_____

_____

_____

_____

_____

_____

_____

_____

_____

_____

_____

_____

_____

_____

_____

_____

_____

_____

_____

_____

_____

_____

_____

I am co-creator

Chapter Ten

Nothingness

"I am peaceful on a consistent basis"
"I dare to experience for myself"
"LIFE is a learning process and I dare to learn"
"My journey is mine and is different than yours"

I am sitting here feeling nothing, nothing at all, just quietness, peace within me. When did it start? I don't remember. I just know that it feels right, feels as it should be. There is peace within. I can hear my own thoughts with no effort. Isn't that how life is meant to be? Peaceful on a consistent basis. No questions asked, no effort made. What an amazing experience, effortless peace within. Shouldn't peace be effortless?

I am blessed with LIFE (Live Intensely Fully Energetically) by the universe. I get up every morning knowing I am in the perfect place to become what I came to earth to be. I feel the spirit that I am vibrate, smile at me. I have this joyful life that I cannot contain within me. I laugh out loud. I love feeling this joy on a daily basis—the joy within.

Imagine. Sit. Take a few deep breaths. I do not lift my chest. I breathe through my chakras, from the sacral all the way up. I connect myself with mother earth and father universe by just breathing deeply. Oh, let the thoughts be. Let them come and go. Who can stop the waves of the ocean? Let the thoughts do what they do, pay attention to

breathing. See how effortless it is, how satisfying. Oxygen fills my lungs, cleansing what needs to be cleansed. I effortlessly expel this breath. I feel it, allowing myself to be absorbed by this breath that comes and go with ease. The air goes in and out, in and out. I am aware of it. I visualise my comfortable life. This breath has been given to me for a purpose, and I am sure that purpose was not suffering or struggling. Love. Peace. Happiness. Joy. I repeat those words as I inhale, as I accept and welcome this life force into me. Inhale. LOVE. Exhale. Inhale. PEACE. Exhale. Inhale. JOY. Exhale. Inhale. HAPPINESS. Exhale. I feel this laughter within me and allow it to be. If this joy comes as windshield washer fluid, I will allow it to run down my cheeks and make my way more clear. Just allow it to be, with no expectations. Do I worry about the next breath not happening every time I take a breath? If I do then I will be not only a really busy person, but full of worries as well, not fun to be around. I take this breath; I do not worry about taking the next breath, it just happens automatically.

We take approximately 23,000 breaths per day. I don't count them or anticipate them. I let my diaphragm and my lungs do what they are meant to do, and I focus on what I do! I Love. I Enjoy. I Embrace LIFE in every single form and shape that it appears to me.

We come to earth in very different forms and shapes. My journey is mine; my path is different than yours.

I remember the only time my mum came to visit. It was her first trip to Canada. She stayed with my sibling in another province and visited me for a week. We were in downtown Edmonton waiting at the bus stop. My mum had ten children, and she manages somehow to be in good shape and not be overweight. At the bus stop, she turns and asks me, "How come people are so overweight here?"

"Why don't you go to the lady and ask her?" I replied.

She didn't appreciate my answer. Does the look, the weight, shape, size of a person define who that person truly is? I stop a moment and thought about the times I judged someone or even myself based on those qualities. Aren't we more than just flesh

and bones? What about the spirit within me, my true self, living in this beautiful physical temple that houses my being?

A house! I just bought a house. I am over super hyper excited. I explore every single room, and as I discover each space, I am amazed how perfectly those rooms have been built. "This builder," I tell myself, "is as smart guy." Large windows face south in spacious rooms. The yard is amazing! All is perfect. I choose which one will be my bedroom, the master bedroom. I bring in my luggage; hang my clothes in the huge walk-in closet the way I want. It is the way I learned from my mum, dad, other relationships over the years—a mixed up collection with no apparent order. I jump on the bed and relax. I feel good to be alive.

But years go by. I become busy doing what I do to keep myself busy. I have no time, or when I have time, I have no energy. I don't feel like cleaning. I don't want to store the luggage sitting in the hallway since my last trip, five years ago. I don't want to donate the clothes hanging in the closet that no longer fit. I don't have time to wash the dirty clothes on the floor. I stop doing laundry

as often as I used to. I just buy new clothes, new underwear, and new t-shirts when nothing is clean. I'm too tired to shower after work, and I don't get up early enough to have time in the morning. And on the weekend, who cares? I'm home alone, why do I need to shower? Deodorant and perfume work just as well. I am amazing at finding ways to avoid doing what needs to be done to feel well.

I came into life, eager to explore—feeling the way I need to feel without self-doubt. A baby who cries, cries; who laughs, laughs with all her heart. The baby just IS. Then I began to grow, started losing that innocence. I slowly changed from the cute little being my parents and siblings welcomed with loving arms and without judgement. I grew up, I was taught from parents, teachers, neighbours, and society what was safe. I was taught how life should be lived. I had to have a reason to cry, and it was never good enough. Laughing alone in a room with the TV off meant I needed serious help. So, I began colouring within those lines. Once in a while, I dared to listen to that infant within me and move just a tiny bit outside of the Safe Zone. I dared to experience for myself, to see what was truly

out there. But they had a name for that, Teenager. I no longer did what I was told to do. "See, she no longer listens to me. She doesn't respect me," they would say. And then the guilt, the shame would send me back to the Safe Zone and I would stay there unhappy, without the energy to embrace and nourish my inner self. I lived someone else's life. I walked on someone else path.

I learned about lack and limitation. I learned about the Safe Zone. I learned about not trusting the voice within. I learned that to be happy, I needed to struggle first because "nothing comes for free." I learned a lot about avoiding daring to be who I want to be.

"Trust the Universe, and the Universe will support you. Let go of beliefs you have been taught about lack and limitations. Dare, LIVE."

"Trust? Trust!? You don't know what you are talking about."

How many times did I hear that quiet voice within me telling me to dare? And how often did the other louder voice tell me to stay within the Safe Zone?

But the debate between those voices meant I was ready. I was asking myself questions. I no longer felt comfortable in the Safe Zone.

"What if there is more?"

Even though the whisper, "Trust the Universe," was soft at the beginning, I practiced listening to it, and it strengthened, became more frequent, clearer.

My niece started walking late, at seventeen months, even though her mum took her first steps at eight months. There is no guaranty that my kids will follow all of my steps. They will choose when they start walking, not when mummy or daddy started walking. They will walk when they feel safe enough to use those two legs. They will stand and take one, two, tens, hundreds, thousands steps. They will be helped at first. Then, they will stand alone. So I DARE. I dare to be myself and to listen to myself, to do what I need to do when the time felt right for me.

My friend, my teacher describes this Daring as using a feather to gently dust myself, dust myself of what I learnt that I no longer want in my life. I am learning to be gentle with myself. Anytime I feel anxious, a "You can't do it Mabelle" pop into my

mind, I breathe through it. Yes, it is as simple as that. Breathing, when I am aware of it is a powerful tool.

Two people are swimming a fast river.

One is going with the flow of the river. Once a while there is an "ouch", and the person continue and still have the energy needed to sometimes swim around bigger rocks, to avoid them. Let call this person Harmony, yes that name sound good, Harmony.

Harmony ends up having few bruises and deep cuts at different parts of her body, but she is still going with the river flow, moving forward regardless of the wounds and scares.

Then we have the other person who, after the 1st "ouch", choose to swim upstream, back to a peaceful section of river with no rocks, back to what he is used to. We hear that person breath louder and louder and funny enough we hear another "ouch". Now here is the question, "I thought those few kilometers were safe, without any rocks, what he knows as being safe; where did that ouch come from?" Why not call him Struggle.

Why the second ouch? Swimming against the flow means that eventually Struggle got tired, decided to take a small break in order to recover some strength. The water is always in motion, perpetual movement. So during his small break, the current carried him downstream. And what is few kilometers down? That rock, that rock where Struggle 1st hurt himself, still at the same place, opening the same wound that started healing. Few swearwords toward himself, the rock, the river and the sun… The old wound is opened; He then remember why he has chosen not to go downstream, so he gather what he has left of strength and energy and swim upstream like an Olympic game athlete. This time, Struggle devises a plan, he will swim as far as possible from the rock, take a short break, and keep swimming upstream. But eventually Struggle tires, rests, and is carried downstream into the same rock. It happens again and again. He spends his time and energy swimming upstream.

So let resume, Struggle didn't move very far, it has no idea what is ahead, passed this 1st rock, what was waiting for him, which gifts, which fantastic experiences he could've been part of, and above all

he is tired and not enjoying at all the swim and the scenery.

Struggle and Harmony, who will learn the most, will have the most experiences, maybe meet the most beautiful river creature, or meet others on the way, who are happy to chat and share their experiences because they still have lot of energy to do so, laughing, yes laughing, they still have enough oxygen and strength to laugh, they are not puffing and coughing and swearing at themselves.

Which one will have a great time?

Maybe Harmony will have more scars than Struggle, but those scars will be experiences Harmony allowed in her LIFE and kept going. Maybe Struggle would've met Harmony if he would've allowed himself to follow the river current. They could've lived happy forever and after. But because Struggle decided to keep going against the flow, it will not happen, and who knows what other LIFE opportunities he missed.

Am I Struggle or Harmony? Who do I want to be?

When I get up every morning, I can choose to swim upstream or downstream. I choose how

I will live that day. What is more important than today, that very special thing I am living right now? When deciding the important events of my day, I must ask myself if everything on this list matters if I die, if my spirit leaves this body tomorrow. I choose. I always choose.

There are no mistakes, LIFE is a learning process, and I DARE to LEARN.

Life is a journey. I Live my LIFE. I bless my LIFE. I Laugh every minute I am here; I AM Alive.

This full moon is incredible.

I am learning to be who I am, to listen to my thoughts, to change my thoughts when they are neither positive nor constructive. I still become more negative when I talk about some of my family members. I become the one who wants to fix them. I get upset at them for not choosing to consciously live their lives. I feel like shouting at them, "Can't you see that it is your life?" Thankfully, those conversations just happen in my head and I stop them, change them. Instead, I send them love and accept who they are. I know our paths are different. It is that difference and uniqueness that brings us

closer, that makes me love them. I can learn from their life choices. I choose my methods of learning: pain, joy, excitement or depression. To love them is to let them choose their own ways. Despite all the love I have for each of them, I am not them, and I don't know what this journey on this planet is for them to learn about. Insisting they do what I believe will make them happy might prevent them from learning what they need to learn the way they need to learn it.

I learn at my own pace, and with love I let my family members learn at their own pace.

I am co-creator

I am co-creator

_____

_____

_____

_____

_____

_____

_____

_____

_____

_____

_____

_____

_____

_____

_____

_____

_____

_____

_____

_____

Chapter Eleven

Who Was I

"In the stillness the answer is revealed"
"Breathing, when I am aware of it is a powerful tool"
"It is for me to open my heart"
"I shift my attention and my intentions"
"I am creating small habits with myself"

Few years ago, in the mist of my LIFE, here was my vision of LIFE. Everything was dark, and that was it, there was no way anyone could convinced me that it was any different.

My Life, I never understood what was happening to me and I worry not being able to change anything even if I knew what was happening.

For some people, life is beautiful… But we all know that this is not true, that God, the Divine, doesn't give everything to everybody, otherwise what will the world be like?

At the beginning when I started learning who I am, I thought to be invincible, nothing, nothing could affect me because I was a goddess.

In fact, I was able to show myself to other as a courageous, smart, strong person, in fact, I wanted to be the one other will be jealous of because of what I had to show. I don't know if I was lying to myself or that I just didn't know myself by then.

Several years went by, and here I am, meeting myself for the 1st time. Today I know a little bit about me, a little about what I like, what I want in my LIFE.

I lived several marking events in my LIFE and never took the time to work on any; I never thought that feelings not taken care of from the past could resurface, so far I have been good in keeping them down. I didn't know that buried feeling can become trigger points that can be awaken from any events or situation.

Go see a psychologist?

"That's for weak people, and I am strong, forget about that, what a silly idea."

Oh yes, I always told myself that with or without a father, with or without mourning my father, I will live well and that will never affect my life. Oh well, I lied to myself.

Slowly by slowly I started learning more about myself, I felt sadness that made me happy because recognizing what is blocking me allow me to release it.

So I learnt that I was weak, that I was playing the strong tough girl just so no one will bother me, so I can keep all my feelings and emotions within.

Inside of me, I was afraid of LIFE, I was afraid of what lay ahead of me, of that uncertain future, I like to control, but the future seems to constantly slip through my fingers.

I also learnt that I am in need of affection, of love, that I need to feel loved all the time.

I finally understood why I couldn't stay more than 6 months in a relationship... because I was afraid of loving, and when I loved I was simply afraid of not being loved the right way, and that I will be hurt at the end anyway. The 1st 3-6 months are the perfect moment, but then the relationship starts going downhill, according to my version; it is when the man is ready to reach for the moon for me, but then when those moments are over, after we made love and the relationship needs to move in a more deep level, I don't feel loved anymore "Why he doesn't call me as often as before?".

I needed to feel loved all the time otherwise I panicked and run away. It was like I always needed proof, proof of being loved. And because I didn't want my partner of the moment to be the one to leave, I will leave him 1ˢᵗ. And here I am feeling sad, letting other, my friends, believe that he let me down and after couple of weeks pretend to other that I was happy without the man.

A father, my father was a strong figure in my life; he was immensely important in my life growing up. I always looked up at him and felt close to him at all time; I knew I could count on him no matter what my siblings or mum will tell him about me misbehaving.

At one point in my life, home, I decided that the daily allowance I was receiving from my parents were no longer enough for my daily needs. I decided to start helping myself in my dad's pants pockets.

He will hang his work cloths in their bedroom and he always had change in the pockets. I will plunge my hand in a pocket and take a hand full of change. He seems to have never noticed.

One evening, just before bedtime, he stopped me as I was getting in the bedroom I shared with my 3 sisters. My heart was pounding, I was ready to faint; he never "cornered" me before. "Mabelle, your siblings told me that you steal money from me. If it is true, I will ask you to stop doing so, but if it is not true, forget that I told you anything", and he went to bed. I had the fear of my life. I never took money from his pocket ever again. I never stole money from him again, because he trusted me. He trusted me that I was able to make the right decision. He didn't yell, spank me or ridiculed me in front of my siblings, but he spoke to me like I was an adult, like I will know what decision to make.

I am so grateful I stopped, because no long after that he got sick. A long disease. I've seen my dad needing a cane to walk, then not being able to remember how to write his own name. He will take the chalk and try to write his own name on the black board and couldn't.

I've seen my dad not able to walk anymore.
I've seen my dad not able to talk anymore.
I've seen my dad not able to feed himself anymore.
I've seen my dad relieve himself where he was.
I've seen my dad not able to sit anymore.

But, he was still my dad. Every morning before leaving to school, I would walk to the bed he was permanently lying on during the day and say "Bye papa, have a good day" and leave to school. And when I was back from school I would walk to that same bed and say "Hello papa".

At the beginning of his disease, he asked me one afternoon to come with him to the land he bought. It had a house being built on it and beside it there was a vegetable garden. We didn't walk that day; instead, I sat at the back of his bicycle and he cycled to the land. We spent much of the afternoon together, but when we came back, mum wasn't happy; she feared that he could've lost his balance and hurt himself and me. He never asked me again to come with him.

I have never been told what was wrong with him; I had no idea what disease affected my dad. There was no explanation. All I knew is that dad walked and talked to me, and now he could no longer do neither.

This love of my life was there
and then not anymore.
He never told me that he loved
me, but I knew he did.
He never gave me a hug, but often he
will hold my head and keep me beside
him while talking to someone.
He never said how important I was to
him, but allowed me to go to work with
him and bought me grapes after lunch.
I had never said good bye to him,
because I still needed a father when he
passed. I had never said good bye.
I refused to talk about my dad to anyone.
I refused to share with anyone the
moment I spent with my dad.
I kept it all to myself.
I kept him all for myself.

Anytime I will be in a relationship, that unfinished business will be triggered. I never wanted anyone, any man to leave me again. Not only will I be the one ending the relationship, but

I will not say good bye. I was not only afraid that the man I was with will fall in love with me, which meant he will leave me without saying goodbye. So, brave as I was, I took the bull by the horn and left, ended up most of my love relationship.

18 years after my dad passing, I wrote him this letter:

"It has been 18 years, four days and several hours that you passed, after two years of being sick, I will say a traumatic two years for me. When all the images, the memories of you that come are the one of when you were sick, I am feeling sad, sad to not have taken advantage of the time I had with you, that gift of time I had with you, because after all, life is an ephemeral gift, like a tulip plant that come out of the soil in spring and dies soon after.

The part that was unfortunate, is that after you were 'gone', I felt guilty, I always felt of not taking advantage of your last moment. I could've asked you more questions, I should've sat at your feet and massage them when you were sick, I should've… The mind just never stops. I was 14 years, 2 months and a day old; I did what I knew at the time, what I was able to do as a teenager.

But, now I am happy that after 18 years, 4 days and several hours, without you being physically present in my life, you my teacher, my daddy, my God on earth, I can finally let go of this life experience, I can finally let go of that experience in my life and just keep the lessons learnt.

There are lot of regrets, lot of 'I could've, should've", but how is that supporting me in my life now? I am learning to fully embrace each and every day, because who knows when it will be my turn to leave this plane, this perishable body and say THANK YOU to this master, this great master that was you, my father.

Thank you to you, you made my childhood full of memories I can cherish. You have always been a father who was present in my life. From checking and making sure that I did all my homework, to

how I was holding my pen and forming my letters.
You were an incredible parent. And that is all I
need, choose to remember when thinking of you.

I love you forever papa"

I am co-creator

_____

_____

_____

_____

_____

_____

_____

_____

_____

_____

_____

_____

_____

_____

_____

_____

_____

_____

_____

_____

_____

_____

_____

_____

_____

_____

_____

_____

_____

_____

_____

_____

_____

_____

_____

_____

_____

_____

_____

_____

_____

I am co-creator

_____

_____

_____

_____

_____

_____

_____

_____

_____

_____

_____

_____

_____

_____

_____

_____

_____

_____

_____

_____

_____

Chapter Twelve

Questions

"I give time to get an answer"
"I am dreaming of an answer"
"The answers ALWAYS come"
"I always have the choice"

Questions come and go.

Some have an answer right away. It seems like the answers were just there, out there, floating in the universe, waiting for only one thing, that someone ask the question. . All excited, here they are in front of the eyes, in the head of the person who asked the question.

The interrogator is satisfied or not, but the question was answered, the job is done.

The only reason for the existence of an answer is to answer a question. The satisfaction of the interrogator is irrelevant. She did her duty, regardless of the interrogator being satisfied or not with her.

Other questions stay without answer, at least which is what the interrogator believes.

Many scenarios can be the reason of it. Let put down few:

-The answers scream, scream loud enough to be heard by the interrogator, but he is "deaf", "deaf" because as soon as he asks a question, another comes up, and another one, one after another.

He is too busy asking question to notice the answers.

He will, finally tell himself: "I never get any answer to my questions"

He will then insist by asking more and more questions. Multitudes of questions, one after another.

Eventually, during his sleep, he will dream of an answer.

This answer is proud, because she accomplished her duty.

He wakes up, knowing that he has the answers to his questions, but says: "That dream was certainly not the answer at my question; this is not the answer I am expecting"

He forgets about it.

He continues his quest for the PERFECT ANSWER.

What's a quest!

He is finally exhausted asking questions and decides to never again ask any question, because answers just seem to hate him or he hates the answer he gets.

A little bit of calm comes back, and with it, a great frustration.

Suddenly all the answers come, one after another. All at once.

He realizes that some answers are related to the questions he has been asking.

He is now to busy, but mostly too discouraged to listen to them and do anything with them.

He let them evaporate, disperse in the universe.

The goal of an answer is to answer questions. When they get no attention, they vanish, they disappear.

-The interrogator asks a question, but right away his attention is focused to a television show, an email that just arrived or a phone call.

He is distracted and merely forgets that he even asked a question.

The answer vanishes.

The interrogator asks a question

She gives time to get an answer. She pays attention to the answers, knowing that they can come in any form and shape, sometimes directly to her, some other time through a friend, a family member, a stranger, a book. They are multitude of choice. But in the silence, she waits, patiently for the answer.

The answer that comes is ALWAYS the good answer at the time when the question is asked. No it couldn't be better.

To accept this answer and to apply it in her LIFE or to ignore it, is the choice of the interrogator.

In the silence I find the answer.

In the stillness the answer is revealed.

I am co-creator

_____

_____

_____

_____

_____

_____

_____

_____

_____

_____

_____

_____

_____

_____

_____

_____

_____

_____

_____

_____

_____

_____

_____

_____

_____

_____

_____

_____

_____

_____

_____

_____

_____

_____

_____

_____

_____

_____

_____

_____

_____

I am co-creator

Printed in the United States
By Bookmasters